SOUTHERN COLORADO
TRAIL GUIDE

Trails Within 50 Miles of Pueblo, Colorado

Nadia N. Brelje

Second Edition
September 2003

Cañon City, Colorado

Copyright ©2003 Nadia N. Brelje
All Rights Reserved

Library of Congress Control Number: 2003094239
ISBN 0-9740249-1-0

All photographs by Nadia N. Brelje with the exception of the Squirrel Creek Lodge photo, courtesy of the Beulah Historical Society

Front cover photo:
Cisneros Trail, San Isabel

Back cover photo:
A foggy, but enchanting, day on
Saint Charles Trail, San Isabel

DEDICATED

To my mother,
Esther M. Brelje

ACKNOWLEDGMENTS

It never occurred to me when I was working on the first edition of this guide that I could possibly do a second edition. But I had so much support, especially from the retailer community, and met so many wonderful people doing the first edition that, in spite of the work involved, I decided to do a second.

New trails are opened while long-established trails are closed, sometimes due to public abuse of private land. Courtesy and responsibility to private landowners are a necessity to preserve access to the trail system, which often lies behind private property. A special thank you goes to the landowners who allow access to public lands through their property, with or without permission.

Since trails keep changing, I'm grateful to those who informed me of changes. I can't mention everyone that has in some way contributed to this second edition, but a few individuals need to be recognized.

After many years of disuse the Millset Trail was reopened to the public the day after I received the first edition from my printer. I immediately went to explore this trail, but lost the path about three miles from the trailhead. I talked my good friend William "Bill" Thousand (who leads many types of trips for the Colorado Mountain Club) into helping me explore the rest of the trail. It took a couple of attempts but we finally made it to the cabin and to Greenhorn Mountain Road. The old blazes on this delightful trail attest to its antiquity. I'm glad the Forest Service was able to get access rights through private rpoperty so the public can once again enjoy this beautiful trail. Bill has also helped me scout other trails in an effort to update this guide.

I had the pleasure of meeting LaVerne Wachob in 2002, a few weeks after her 80th birthday. This delightful, energetic and young "39"-year-old told me the history of the Wachob Trail, named after her husband, John "Jack" Alvin Wachob. This history gives personality to a delightful trail.

Also, thanks go to my special friend Barb Moy, who traveled from Montana to Colorado to visit me and to hike some of the local trails. Time was short so we hiked even when the weather was rainy and foggy. A hike on the Saint Charles Trail from CO 165 resulted in the photo on the back cover of this guide. Ordinarily, indoor projects are done on a rainy day. But we decided to hike to Saint Charles Peak anyway as long as we felt safe on the trail. The rain soon stopped but the fog continued, resulting in one of the most mystical and enchanting hikes I've ever done. I'm grateful for Barb's willingness to go on this trip in spite of the weather.

My deepest thanks go to my editor and dear friend Loma Huh, whose talent with the English language never ceases to amaze me.

I'm again thankful for having been blessed with a beautiful mother who encouraged me to do this book. She passed away in March 1997, before the first edition was complete, but her spirit guides me every day.

Enjoy your outdoor experience, and thank God for the beauty He has created for all of us.

CONTENTS

INTRODUCTION 1

FOR A BETTER OUTING 2
   About This Guide 2
   Where Are You Going? 2
   What to Take and Why 3
   Courtesy 5
   Dangers/Hazards 6
      Plants 6
      Animals 6
      Hypothermia 9
      Heat Exhaustion and Heat Stroke 10
      Altitude Sickness 10
      Lightning 11
   Restrooms and Washing 11
   Campfires 11
   Colorado Outdoor Recreation Search and Rescue Card 12
   Getting Lost 12
   Disclaimer 14
   Volunteer 14
   When to Hike 14

LIFE ZONES 15

HISTORY AND GEOLOGY 17
   Beulah Area 17
   Cañon City Area 21
   Rye Area 25
   San Isabel Area 25

TRAIL DESCRIPTIONS 28

   BEULAH AREA
      Pueblo Mountain Park Trails 28
         Mace Trail and Lookout Point Trail 30
         North Ridge Trail and Devil's Canyon Trail ... 31
         Tower Trail 33
         Camp Burch and Ranger Trail 35

    South Creek Trail #1321. 35
    Squirrel Creek Trail #1384 37
    Second Mace Trail #1322. 42
    Dome Rock Trail #1387 43

CAÑON CITY AREA
    Arkansas Riverwalk—Cañon City 45
    Fremont Peak. 46
    McIntyre Hills 49
    Trails from Temple Canyon Road 50
        B.F. Rockafellow Ecology Park 50
        Temple Canyon Trail 52
        The Tights 55
    Trails from the Oak Creek Grade Road
    (Fremont County Road 143). 57
        East Pierce Gulch. 57
        Lion Canyon—Highline Trail #1329 61
        Stultz Trail #1334 61
        Stultz Trail—Forest Road 348 65
        Tanner Trail #1333 65
    Trails from Fremont County Road 9 70
        Red Canyon Park 71
        Sand Gulch Area 71
            Sand Gulch Trails 72
            The Gallery Trails 75
            The Bank 75

COLORADO SPRINGS AREA
    Clear Spring Ranch Trail 77
    Fountain Creek Regional Park 78
    Bear Creek Regional Park. 80
    Trails from Gold Camp Road/High Drive Area 81
        Bear Creek Trail #666 83
        Saint Mary's Falls Trail #624 85
        Seven Bridges Trail (North Cheyenne Trail) #622. . . 86
    Waldo Canyon Trail #640 90

FLORENCE AREA
    Newlin Creek Trail #1335. 93

OPHIR CREEK—BIGELOW DIVIDE (FAIRVIEW) AREA
    Trails from Ditch Creek Road 97
        Left Hand Fork Trail #1325 97
        Silver Circle Trail #1323 98

    Second Mace Trail #1322 101
    Middle Creek Trail #1328 103
    Saint Charles Trail from Ophir Creek Road 106

PENROSE AREA
    Aiken Canyon Preserve 107
    Trails from Upper Beaver Creek Road
      (Fremont County Road 132) 109
        Beaver Creek Trail 110
        Trail Gulch Trail 114
        Table Mountain Trail 115
    Holbert Trail 118

PUEBLO AREA
    Pueblo Trails 123
        University Park Trail 123
        Pueblo Mall Trail 123
        Fountain Creek Trail 124
        Runyon Lake Trail 124
        Arkansas Riverwalk—Pueblo 125
        Arkansas River Trail East 126
        Arkansas River Trail West 126
        Pueblo Boulevard—Northern Avenue Trails 128
    Pueblo Reservoir Trails 129
        Arkansas Point Trails 130
        Conduit Nature Trail 131
        Miscellaneous Trails 133

RYE AREA
    Apache Falls Trail #1311 134
    Bartlett Trail #1310 139
    Greenhorn Trail #1316 142
    Millset Trail #1317 145

SAN ISABEL AREA
    Snowslide Trail #1318 148
    Cisneros Trail #1314—
      Marion Mine Trail and Saint Charles Trail Access . . . 151
    Marion Mine Trail 154
    Saint Charles Trail #1326
      (with Side Trip to Marion Lake) 157
    San Carlos Trail #1320 and Natural Arch 162
    South Creek Trail #1321 166
    Wachob Trail #1319 167

WALSENBURG AREA
    Hogback Trail 169
    Martin Lake Trail 170

WETMORE AREA
    Lewis Creek—Highline Trail #1331 171
    Newlin Creek Trail #1335 175
    Rudolph Mountain Trail #1327.................. 175

APPENDIX A
Ten Essentials and Other Useful Items 178

APPENDIX B
Backpacking Equipment 181

APPENDIX C
Maps Used in This Guide 183
Map Sources 184

APPENDIX D
Information Sources 185

BIBLIOGRAPHY 188

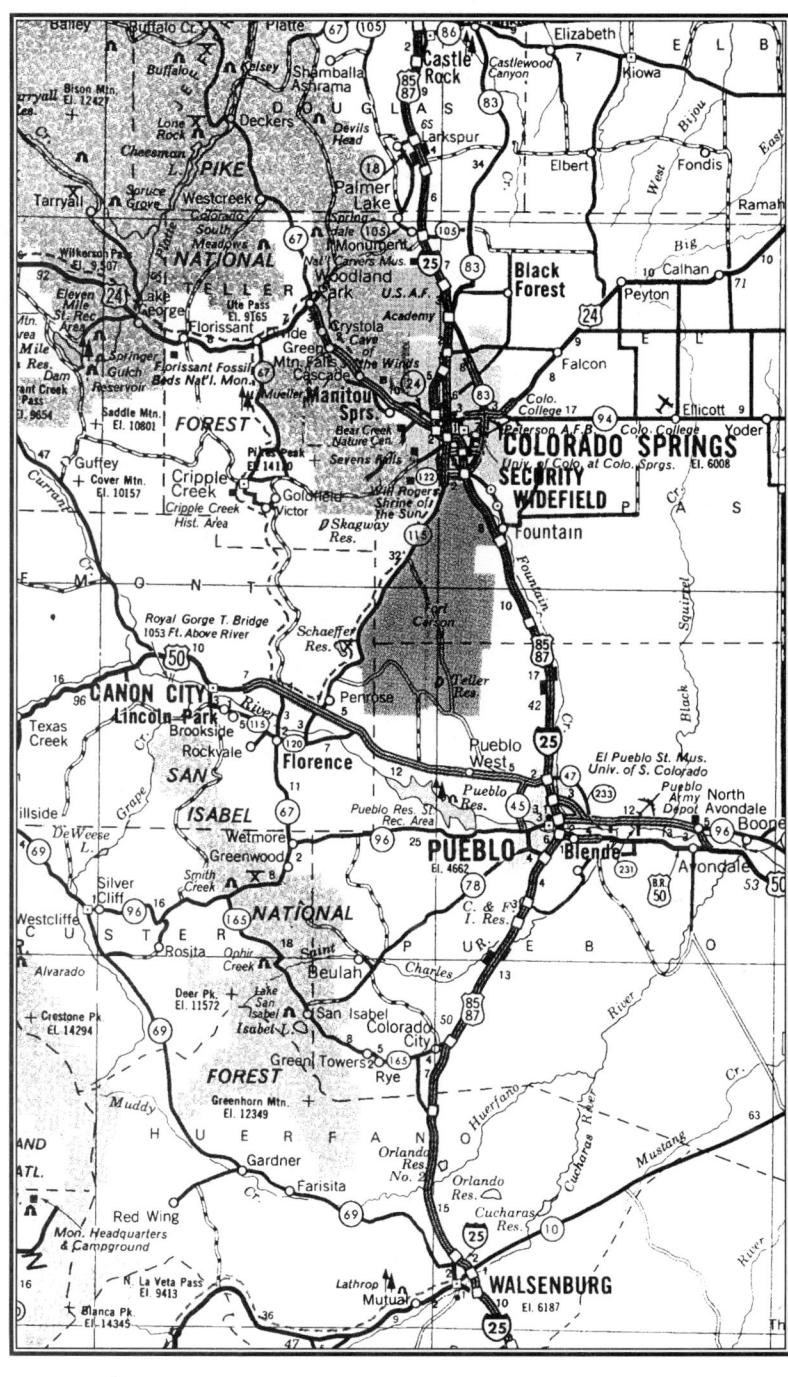

INTRODUCTION

Has cabin fever struck? Do you want a little fresh air and perhaps some much-needed exercise? You hate to drive and the dogs on your block make hiking from your home impossible? Don't despair. The southern Front Range offers more than 250 miles of trails within a 50-mile drive of Pueblo, Colorado. Trails along the Arkansas River and Fountain Creek are only a few minutes away from anywhere in Pueblo. The state park and the state wildlife area at Pueblo Reservoir offer a few established trails plus many acres to explore off-trail. Beulah offers an extensive trail system through Pueblo Mountain Park and the adjacent San Isabel National Forest. Cañon City, Colorado Springs, Florence, "Fairview" (Ophir Creek—Bigelow Divide area), Penrose, Rye, San Isabel, Walsenburg, and Wetmore have a variety of trails nearby.

All these areas have trails for the young and the old, for the physically fit and the couch potato, and for a short 30-minute hike or an all-day excursion. Trails in some areas are suitable for backpacking. If you have young children, hiking is an excellent way to introduce them to the world of nature.

If you're planning more than a half-hour round trip from your car, take a daypack with essentials, such as raingear, water, snacks, map(s), and compass. Read the "For a Better Outing" section and refer to Appendix A for a list of the ten essentials.

You are responsible for your own safety, so be prepared.

FOR A BETTER OUTING

ABOUT THIS GUIDE

With the exception of Ophir Creek—Bigelow Divide (Fairview), the guide is organized alphabetically by cities. Terms such as left and right have been used, but must be observed with caution. You have to be traveling the trail in the same direction as described for these directions to be meaningful. North, south, east, and west are included to assist with trail locations.

Odometer readings for the road directions may vary slightly with different vehicles but are given as accurately as possible. Difficulty of trails is based on elevation gain/loss and distance. Elevation gain (or loss) is not necessarily the difference between the highest and lowest elevations. Several trails have a significant intervening loss of elevation that must be regained. These elevation changes have been included in the elevation gain figures.

Use the miles and elevation changes as a guide to the trail difficulty. The higher the number of miles and the greater the elevation change, the more difficult the trail will be. However, the most difficult trails in this guide will be easy for the physically fit, while the easiest trails may seem difficult for those less fit.

When selecting a trail to hike, consider your physical condition and know your limitations. If you've never hiked, start with the easier trails such as the Arkansas River trail system at the Nature Center in Pueblo, the Bear Creek or Fountain Creek Regional Parks near Colorado Springs, or the Arkansas Riverwalk in Cañon City. These trails require little or no equipment, and help is close if you should have a problem. Longer and steeper trails do not have to be hiked the entire length. Trails at higher elevations will be cooler. Hike your selected trail only as far as you feel able, within the time you've allowed, and enjoy what nature has to offer.

WHERE ARE YOU GOING?

Before leaving on a hike, **always tell someone where you are going and when you expect to return. Don't hike alone.** If you insist on hiking alone and not telling someone where you're headed, at least leave a note in a conspicuous place indicating your whereabouts, in case authorities are asked to gain access to your home because someone is looking for you.

WHAT TO TAKE AND WHY

The following discussion is for backcountry trails, where access to help may be many miles away. Each piece of recommended equipment is important if a situation arises in which it will be needed. Quite possibly you could hike many enjoyable miles with no problems, having only appropriate footgear and water; however, this is extremely risky. Refer to Appendix A for a complete list of the ten essentials, other recommended gear, and first-aid supplies. Make sure you have all the appropriate gear before setting off on a mountain hike.

Wearing suitable footgear (usually hiking boots) is the best insurance against a sprained or broken ankle. Any comfortable walking shoe is adequate for asphalt and concrete trails, but a hiking boot with a Vibram sole is best for the mountain trails. Many lightweight hiking boots are available on the market today. If you have weak ankles, select boots with supportive leather at the ankle bone and avoid boots that have the less supportive cloth construction.

When you shop for boots, try on the boots with the socks you plan to wear when hiking. If the boots are not comfortable in the store—keep shopping. Wear two pairs of socks with your hiking boots—a thin inner pair and a heavier wool outer pair.

Make sure the boots you buy are long enough. You don't want the end of your toes hitting the boot when hiking downhill. Cut your toenails. Toes and toenails can become very painful and can turn black if they are forced into the end of a too-short boot.

Break in your boots on several short hikes. If you feel a hot spot, the first sign of a blister forming, stop immediately and apply moleskin. If a blister does form, do not put the moleskin directly on the blister, but cut a hole in the moleskin large enough to go around the blister. Even old boots can sometimes cause blisters. Always treat immediately, as the excruciating pain of a blister can ruin an otherwise wonderful hike.

Take plenty of water—at least one quart per person, two quarts each for hot weather. On hot days add a few ice cubes to your water bottle. If you're hiking in the cool winter weather, start with warm or hot water. Since many creeks and streams flow intermittently do not depend upon these sources for replenishing your water supply. In addition, **ALL backcountry water MUST be treated before drinking (see "Animals—giardia" section, page 6)**. Include in your supplies a steel cup for heating water. Hot water can warm a cold hiker and safely refill a water bottle when backcountry water is available.

How long you plan to hike will determine how much food you should take. Quick-energy trail mixes, carrot sticks, and dried fruits, such as raisins, are excellent for short hikes. Take a sandwich for longer outings. If you take oranges or bananas, you must pack out the peelings. Be aware that bananas can get smashed and very messy in a pack!

Raingear (poncho) on a longer hike is a must for those afternoon showers that develop so quickly (see "Hypothermia" section). Dress in layers (T-shirt, wool sweater) and include a windbreaker jacket. Shorts are more comfortable in warm weather but won't give protection against scratches and sunburn. If you prefer to hike in shorts, include rain/wind pants that zip down the sides so you don't have to remove your boots to put them on. Take a wide-brimmed hat for sun protection and a wool stocking cap in case the weather turns bad. Gloves can be a most welcome item for cold weather and for protection against sharp rocks. In the fall, wear orange so hunters don't mistake you for a five-point buck. Keep a close eye on the weather. If you haven't brought enough clothing to protect you from impending bad weather, return to your car.

Use the San Isabel National Forest or Pike National Forest maps when appropriate to get a good overview of the area. The numbers associated with the trail descriptions refer to these maps. Trail signs may have only these numbers, so add them to your USGS topographic (topo) maps. Having and knowing how to use a compass and a topo map can keep you going in the right direction. Each trail description lists the topo map(s) needed. A complete list of all maps used in this guide and suggestions of where to buy them are in Appendix C.

Tweezers are great for removing thorns from that cactus you just sat on or grabbed by accident. They come in handy for slivers and ticks, also. Insect repellent is a nice thing to have, especially during the spring and early summer tick season (see "Animals—ticks" section).

Wear a watch so you have some idea of how long you've been out and how many hours of daylight are left. Do you have enough time to do what you planned? If the return trip is downhill it'll take less time to get back to your car than it took to do the uphill. If you're two hours up, figure a bit more than an hour down.

A bandana can be used as a handkerchief, washcloth, bandage, sling, or sunshade for the back of your neck. A piece of tinfoil can make a signal mirror, a water collector, or a hat. A piece of one-eighth-inch nylon rope is useful for repairing equipment, for shoelaces, or for the support to a makeshift shelter using a poncho or a space blanket as a tent.

Your gear should include a flashlight with extra batteries and bulb, sunglasses, sunscreen, pocketknife, matches in a waterproof container, a candle or other firestarter, and a first-aid kit. Lip balm, facial tissue, and toilet paper always seem to be needed.

If you're a photographer you'll want to include a camera and some film, or a camcorder and tape. A pair of lightweight binoculars are fun and useful. Fishermen will want to take the appropriate gear.

If you're backpacking you'll need all the gear for a day hike, plus such things as a tent, a sleeping bag, a mat, and cooking utensils. Appendix B gives a complete list of nice things to have on an overnight trip. If you've never backpacked you might consider renting or borrowing equipment for the first few trips. Then if you do decide to invest in your own equipment you'll be a much smarter shopper.

COURTESY

Many trails cross or are close to private property. If you do not respect private property the trail access could be closed. Leave all gates opened or closed as you found them. Please be considerate.

Tossed candy bar wrappers, used facial tissues, tin cans, and disposable diapers become unsightly along the trail and at a campsite. Banana and orange peels decompose at an incredibly slow rate. **If you packed it in, pack it out.** Carry a small plastic bag for all trash you have or any you find. Leave the wilderness cleaner than you found it.

When hiking with others, leave about ten feet between hikers. Too many followers see nothing but the boots and buttocks of the person in front of them. Every person on the hike needs to be aware of the surroundings (see "Getting Lost" section). You'll see more if you stay off the heels of the person in front of you. But don't wander off alone; stay with the group.

Trails may be shared with motorcycles, mountain bikers, and horseback riders. Move to the side of the trail to let these users pass. If possible get off the trail downhill when horses come along. Allow faster hiking parties to pass. Give everyone a warm smile. Others have just as much right to be on the trail as you do. To the best of your ability answer any questions others may have.

Take only pictures; leave only footprints. Respect nature (see "Plants—wildflowers" and "Animals—pets" sections).

DANGERS/HAZARDS

Plants

Poison ivy is widespread and can ruin your outing. Even contact with the dead leaves and the smoke from burning poison ivy can cause an allergic reaction. Learn to recognize the plant so you can avoid it. Poison ivy is distinguished by three glossy leaflets. The plant has greenish-white flowers, and its white berries grow in clusters. In the fall the leaves turn color ranging from yellow to orange and brilliant red. It may grow as a small plant, a vine, or a shrub. The skin rash produced by contact with poison ivy is characterized by redness, blisters, swelling, and intense burning and itching. A headache and a high fever may develop and the victim may become very ill. The rash usually begins within a few hours after exposure, but may be delayed for 48 hours. First aid requires removing contaminated clothing. Thoroughly wash all exposed areas with soap and water, followed by rubbing alcohol. If the rash is mild, apply calamine or other soothing skin lotion. For severe reactions, or if there is a known history of previous sensitivity, seek medical advice.

Don't pick the wildflowers. Leave them for others to enjoy. If you pick the flowers they can't produce seed for next year's blossoms. Picked wildflowers wilt quickly. Besides, picking and digging up some wildflowers is illegal. Don't take shortcuts between switchbacks. Off-trail hiking kills the vegetation and causes erosion. Don't chop down green standing trees and don't cut boughs for a bed.

Leave the land and plants as nature intended—wild.

Animals

All water from creeks, streams, ponds, and lakes **must** be boiled for at least a minute, or filtered, before drinking to prevent sickness caused by giardia (a protozoan) and other unseen beasts. Giardia causes severe diarrhea, intestinal cramping, vomiting, and loss of appetite and weight. Giardiasis, the illness, must be treated by a doctor. Chemical tablets can be used in an emergency but are not always effective, and they make the water taste bad.

Bears have been seen in many areas along these trails. Watch for their signs, such as tracks, droppings, claw markings on trees, and overturned rocks, especially at ant hills. Make noise (talk, sing, or use a bear bell) along the trail to alert a bear to your presence, allowing the bear time to retreat before it sees you. Bears seem to be more aggressive toward those wearing scented deodorant, hair spray, and cosmetics.

Bear claw markings on aspen tree—Apache Falls Trail

If you should encounter a bear, **stay calm**. If the bear hasn't seen you, calmly leave the area while talking aloud to let the bear discover your presence. If the bear sees you, back away slowly, avoiding direct eye contact. Give the bear plenty of room to retreat, especially if cubs are present. Speaking softly may reassure the bear that you mean no harm. Don't run—the bear might think you're worth chasing, and you can't win that race. The bear may try to identify you by standing upright and moving closer. It may charge to within a few feet before withdrawing. If attacked, fight back with anything you have available, including your bare hands. Bear encounters are surprisingly few, but remain alert to the possible danger.

A <u>mountain lion</u> encounter is even more rare than a bear encounter. Follow the same suggestions as for a bear encounter but additionally do all you can to appear larger. Raise your arms. If you're wearing a jacket, open it wide. If attacked, try to remain standing while fighting back. **Never run** as that might stimulate the lion's instinct to chase and attack.

Rocks and bluffs at the lower (below 8,000') elevation trails may harbor <u>rattlesnakes</u>. Carry a snake-bite kit if you hike in rattlesnake country. Rattlesnakes strike only when threatened. Watch for them and keep a safe distance if you encounter one. If reaching for a handhold on the rocks, look first to make sure a rattlesnake isn't sunning itself on the rock. If bitten, stay calm. Wash the wound with soap and water or antiseptic. Firmly wrap a cloth above the bite. Be careful that you don't cut off the circulation. You should be able to slip a finger under the wrap. Splint the limb to immobilize it, and seek medical attention. Treat for shock.

Non-poisonous snakes have round pupils and no fangs. Poisonous snake fangs make one or two puncture wounds. Bullsnakes look very much like rattlers, but they have no rattle and no poison.

Do not handle <u>wild animals</u> or feed them since they may transmit such diseases as bubonic plague and Hantavirus. If an animal behaves strangely it may have rabies. If you develop puzzling symptoms after an outdoor excursion, contact your doctor.

Even if using insect repellent for <u>ticks</u>, check yourself regularly. Tucking your pants into your socks and your shirt into your pants helps prevent tick bites. Wearing light–colored clothing during the tick season makes it easier to spot ticks. Ticks usually take several hours to become imbedded. If a tick does become imbedded, the American Red Cross *Standard First Aid* manual recommends covering the tick with heavy oil (salad, mineral, or machine) to close its breathing pores. The tick may disengage immediately or within a half hour. When disengaged, gently remove the tick with tweezers. Wash the area with soap and water. More recent methods suggest removing the tick by grasping it close to the skin with a pair of fine-tip tweezers or by using a sterile needle as you would remove a sliver. Then apply an antibiotic ointment.

Cattle may be encountered on some of the trails. Usually they will run away from you, but try to hike around them if they block the trail. Don't chase or spook cattle because bulls or cows with calves could charge. Usually cattle won't hassle people, so don't hassle them. The farmers and ranchers will also appreciate your consideration.

Your pets are best left at home, but if Rover really wants to hike, know the rules and restrictions, if any, where you plan to hike. For example, you cannot take your dog on the nature trails in the Bear Creek or Fountain Creek Regional Parks. In city and state parks that allow dogs, a leash no longer than six feet is usually required. Dogs are permitted in wilderness areas but must be on a leash at all times. If National Forests and Bureau of Land Management lands are not wilderness areas, dogs are allowed to run free, but always take a leash in case your dog needs to be restrained. If pets aren't controlled at all times by their owners, additional rules and restrictions may be established. Noncompliance to regulations usually results in a fine. Keeping your dog under control also helps prevent a nasty encounter with a porcupine or skunk. No wild animal, including birds and squirrels, wants to be chased by your dog. Remove dog feces from the trail. Feces on a trail are a nuisance and unsightly. Off the trail they become great fertilizer.

Hypothermia

Hypothermia is a subnormal temperature of the body's core and occurs when the body loses heat faster than it can produce it. When Colorado's dry climate changes from a sunny, glorious day to a suddenly chilling, rainy and windy storm, exposure can cause hypothermia in minutes. Exhaustion also can aggravate exposure to cold. Hypothermia can cause one to freeze to death in 50° F weather.

Signs of hypothermia are complaints of cold, shivering, difficulty using hands, apathy, and poor decisions. If the victim continues to be exposed to the conditions causing the hypothermia, there will be confusion, slurred speech, sleepiness, and further loss of coordination. Walking becomes difficult. Severe signs are unresponsiveness with weak pulse and respiration. Shivering stops and physical collapse results. Watch for hypothermia in yourself and your fellow hikers. Victims may deny there is a problem. Believe the symptoms observed and not what the victim is saying.

Prevent hypothermia by carrying several layers of clothing that can be put on **before** the problem arises. If your feet are cold, put on a hat to reduce loss of body heat through your head. Always carry raingear and use it **before** getting wet. Eating helps the body to generate heat. **Hypothermia is the biggest danger** on an outing—not bears, lions, or rattlesnakes.

Heat Exhaustion and Heat Stroke

Heat exhaustion is the opposite of hypothermia; thus, heat is gained faster than it can be lost. Signs are pale skin color, profuse sweating, and skin temperature normal or cool. Symptoms are nausea, weakness, dizziness, thirst, and headache. Get the victim into the shade and give plenty of water or sports drinks in sips. Resume activity only when signs and symptoms are completely gone.

A worsening condition of heat exhaustion is heat stroke, which can be fatal. The skin may be red, dry, and hot. Treat as in heat exhaustion but additionally apply a cool, moist cloth to head and neck, and fan the victim. Seek medical help for heat stroke victims.

Drinking plenty of water or sports drinks is the best preventative measure. Don't wait until you're thirsty to drink. If you're thirsty you're already a quart low on water. In the hot summer, hike in the cooler morning or evening hours. Take frequent rest breaks in shaded areas. Adjust your clothing.

Altitude Sickness

High altitude sickness probably won't be a problem for most of the hikes in this book unless you're a lowlander planning to climb Greenhorn Mountain or Saint Charles Peak, or you're in very poor physical condition and hiking beyond your abilities. People from near sea level may wish to acclimate for a couple of days in the local communities before hiking to higher altitudes. If out of condition you should begin on the easy trails.

Signs of altitude sickness are headache, nausea, dizziness and shortness of breath. If symptoms persist or seem to worsen, high altitude pulmonary edema may occur. High altitude pulmonary edema can kill. The only cure is to seek lower elevations.

Eating high-energy foods, drinking plenty of fluids (no alcohol), and hiking at a more moderate pace are good preventative measures.

Lightning

You don't have to be on a ridge to see trees split and charred by lightning; lightning strikes anywhere. Of course the worst places to be in a lightning storm are on a ridge or in a high meadow. Most lightning strikes hit high points on cliffs or peaks, a lone or tall tree, or you if you're the tallest object around.

If you're caught in a thunder and lightning storm, get off the ridges. If you hear buzzing in the rocks or if the hair on your head, neck, arms, or legs begins to stand up, you're in prime territory for a lightning strike. Seek shelter in the thick woods, if possible. Be wary of shallow caves as lightning can travel down a cliff into the shallow cave. If you must stay in the open, crouch down with your arms around your knees. Lay that metal walking stick or photography tripod well away from you. And don't forget to put on your poncho if the lightning storm carries moisture.

The obvious preventative measure is to keep a sharp eye on the weather. If it looks threatening, seek shelter or return to your car.

RESTROOMS AND WASHING

The backcountry trails have no facilities, so human wastes must be decomposed by nature. Select a spot at least 200 feet from water and trails. With your boot, a stick, or a stone, dig a hole no deeper than eight inches. Try to keep the top layer of sod intact. Use only biodegradable toilet paper (or burn the paper if you have a campfire, or carry it out in a small plastic bag). Cover excrement and tissue with loose soil. Replace the sod and add a few needles, twigs, or a loose rock to the top. Nature will do the rest.

Don't pollute natural water sources with soap. Use only biodegradable soaps, wash in a container of water, and carry it away from the source for disposal.

CAMPFIRES

Keep campfires small and use primarily for warmth. Use a small stove instead to cook those fish you just caught. Avoid building a new fire ring if one has already been established. Burn only dead wood. Keep the fire attended at all times and make sure it is **dead out** when you leave. Don't build a fire on a windy day or when fire danger is high.

COLORADO OUTDOOR RECREATION SEARCH AND RESCUE CARD (CORSAR)

If you have a current fishing or hunting license, or a registered boat, ATV, or snowmobile, you have already paid a twenty-five-cent fee for search and rescue. If you do not have one of these licenses or registrations, spend the three dollars per year ($12.00 for 5 years) to purchase a CORSAR card. This is not insurance, but rather a way of funding search and rescue teams in Colorado. Search and rescue missions will be conducted whether or not a person has a license, registration, or card, but if the person has paid this fee, any money spent by the county can be reimbursed from the search and rescue fund rather than from the victim or victim's family. Any money not needed for search and rescue reimbursements is used for training and equipment for search and rescue volunteers.

CORSAR cards can be purchased at the Colorado Trail Foundation office, 710 North 10th Street, Golden, Colorado 80401; or from the Colorado Department of Local Affairs, 222 South Sixth Street, Room #409, Grand Junction, CO 81501; or with a credit card by calling 970-248-7310. For a complete list of vendors call 970-248-7310 or visit the Department of Local Affairs Web site at www.state.co.us/searchandrescue.

GETTING LOST

Every effort has been made to give complete and accurate trail descriptions, **but you can still get lost**. Pay attention to your surroundings. At some point in time you may not know exactly where you are, but you should know how to get back to your vehicle. Daydreaming on the trail can lead to missed junctions or ending up on a game trail. Most people reasonably physically fit can hike a mile in 30 minutes with little or no elevation gain. When elevation gain is added, a good rule of thumb is 1.5 miles per hour plus 750 vertical feet per hour. If the trail is very steep, rocky and/or wet, add more time. A mile in adverse conditions can seem much longer than a mile. But consider that a physically fit person, daydreaming for 15 minutes, could end up 0.5 mile off in the wrong direction. **Stay alert!**

Many trails have markers that come in an assortment of styles and colors. Any trail marker makes you happy because you know you're not lost. A single trail may have a combination of markers that may include plastic tags (blue, pink, red, yellow, or orange), cairns, metal strips with a red tip, metal diamonds (blue or orange), or tree blazes (a short notch over a long notch in the tree's bark). If it's manmade or looks manmade, it's probably a trail marker. Many trails have helpful signs if vandals haven't destroyed them. Carry plastic ribbon to tag overgrown trails. Your markers can be removed on the return trip.

If you do get lost, don't panic. Sit down. Relax. Think back to where you've been. Trails often follow ridges or a stream in a canyon. Has the trail been following along a hillside? Hopefully, you've been tracking your progress on a topo map. That makes it much easier to orient yourself should you stray from the main trail. If you've followed a side trail, don't attempt to bushwhack through the woods to regain the main trail. Retrace your steps on the side trail until you return to the main trail.

If you're completely turned around but want to try to hike out, take the easiest route so you don't get hurt in addition to being lost. If you find a stream, follow it downstream. That usually leads to civilization. Be leery of going down into an unknown canyon or gorge that may trap you.

If the weather is turning nasty, there is not enough daylight to hike out, or you are hurt, seek shelter while awaiting rescue. If you've followed the rules, someone will soon be looking for you. If you just left a note it may take much longer. It's worth repeating—tell someone your plans!

Make a shelter using your poncho or a space blanket. Gather nearby firewood for a small campfire. Don't lose sight of your pack and shelter! The standard SOS is three signals of any kind repeated at regular intervals. Use a whistle instead of yelling. Or use a mirror, shiny knife blade, or tin foil to flash a signal. Build a fire in a clearing, if possible, and add some green boughs during the day to create lots of smoke.

If you can stay warm, dry, and out of the wind, your chances of survival are excellent. Always take the recommended gear on your mountain hikes (see "What to Take and Why" section).

If you hike with children, keep them in sight. And as a precaution, teach them to stay put (affectionately called "hug a tree") if they do get separated from you. Put a whistle on a string around their neck and make sure they know the SOS signal. Time can be an eternity to a lost child. Teach them to sing their favorite nursery rhyme a couple of times between SOS signals. Re-emphasize "hugging" that tree.

DISCLAIMER

Since hiking in the backcountry is not without danger, each individual must be fully prepared for the activity planned. Most people do not get lost, but trails do get overgrown or rerouted, trails and bridges get washed out, and signs disappear. Additionally, individual interpretations of trail descriptions may be different than intended by the author. **You are responsible for yourself** while engaging in any outdoor activity.

VOLUNTEER

Building and maintaining outdoor facilities requires people and money. Volunteer your time or money to the Forest Service, the Bureau of Land Management, or the Division of Wildlife (see Appendix D for addresses and phone numbers). Volunteers are needed to build and maintain trails, erect signs and fences, revegetate wildlife habitat, and construct shelters, tables, and restrooms. Other options include doing office work or assisting in wildlife research. Your efforts are repaid with a sense of pride for a job well done and better facilities to enjoy.

WHEN TO HIKE

The trails at lower elevations are superb in the cooler months of spring and fall, but they can be enjoyed any time of year. In winters with minimal snow, many trails are hikable, but watch for icy patches that may occur where water crosses the trails. In the spring or after heavy rain showers, some trails with creek crossings may have limited hiking due to high water runoff. In the fall the aspens turn to gold, creating one of nature's truly wonderful displays of color. In any season the fresh air invigorates the body and soul. So dust off those hiking boots and go see what's in "them thar hills."

Think Safety! Think Fun! Enjoy!

LIFE ZONES

Topography and climatic factors influence life zones. Elevation influences temperature and moisture, which in turn control the types of plants and animals found in a zone. Higher elevations are cooler and wetter. North-facing slopes are shady and thus wetter than the sunny and drier south-facing slopes. Life zones are not clear cut, so plants and animals characteristic to one zone may also be found in another neighboring zone, and micro-ecosystems may exist in some areas.

Studying the life zones and the plant and animal communities that exist in each can add much to the enjoyment of an outing and will certainly increase your knowledge of the natural world. Occasionally include a field guide for your special interest in your daypack so you can learn more about the wildflowers, trees, birds, mammals, or geology.

The plants and animals of Colorado are divided into five characteristic life zones. The following is a brief description of each. Most of the trails in this guide are in the Transition (Foothills) and Canadian (Montane) Zones.

The Alpine Zone, represented in the Wet Mountains by Greenhorn Mountain, North Peak, and Saint Charles Peak, begins at 11,500'. This harsh and delicate ecosystem is devoid of trees, and summer is very short. The sparse vegetation includes grasses, lichens, and beautiful displays of wildflowers including alpine forget-me-nots. Small birds and mammals call the alpine tundra home. Bighorn sheep frequent this zone.

The Hudsonian (Subalpine) Zone is a narrow band at timberline between 11,000' and 11,500'. Heavy snows and high winds stunt and twist the subalpine fur, bristlecone pine, and Englemann spruce into odd shapes. Animals residing here include elk and snowshoe hare.

The Canadian (Montane) Zone between 8,000' and 11,000' includes aspen, ponderosa and lodgepole pine, and Douglas fir at the lower elevations. Higher elevations will have Englemann spruce, limber pine, and subalpine fir. In spring, summer, and early fall, wildflowers abound including columbine, Indian paintbrush, fairy slipper, fairy trumpet, golden banner, penstemons, and wild iris. Mule dear, beaver, and porcupine frequent this zone.

The Transition (Foothills) Zone lies between 5,500' and 8,000'. Scrub oak, Rocky Mountain juniper, ponderosa pine, and Douglas fir grow on the hillsides while cottonwood, blue spruce, alder, and willows grow along the streams. Abert's squirrels may be seen gathering food among the ponderosa pines.

The Upper Sonoran (Plains) Zone, represented by the Pueblo Reservoir trails, comprises the eastern plains of Colorado with elevations between 3,500' and 5,500'. This zone has short grass prairies, yucca, cactus, pinyon pine, and juniper. Animals frequenting this zone include coyote, prairie dogs, skunk, antelope, rattlesnakes, and many species of birds.

HISTORY AND GEOLOGY

Oftentimes a trail passes an old structure or an interesting geologic feature, or the trail may be the remnants of an old road. Your curiosity begins asking questions about bygone days or about the geologic formation. When appropriate, some history and geology are included with the trail descriptions. This chapter is not intended to be a comprehensive discussion on all the history and geology in the area, but rather a collection of additional interesting facts and stories. Further reading suggestions are included in the bibliography.

BEULAH AREA

Carhart Influence

Beulah was the setting for the ideas and involvement of several farsighted citizens from Pueblo in developing the first recreational use of our National Forests.

Arthur H. Carhart reported for duty at the Rocky Mountain District Headquarters in Denver, Colorado, on March 1, 1919, as the first landscape architect to be hired by the National Forests. The plan he developed in 1920 faced major opposition from the National Park Service, which thought Parks were for recreation and National Forests were for commercial development. Carhart advocated preserving nature and spectacular scenery for the enjoyment of the general public rather than parceling out prime areas to special groups. His recreation development plan has become a model for plans that have followed, and many of his proposals have become policy.

During World War I foreign travel was restricted. Railroads and travel agencies campaigned to "See America First." People had more leisure time, and more people could afford an automobile. Citizens along the Front Range began to agitate for recreational developments in the nearby National Forests.

In 1918 the Pueblo Commerce Club, under the leadership of Pete A. Gray, asked Supervisor Al G. Hamel of the San Isabel National Forest if the Service would install camp and picnic facilities on Squirrel Creek at Beulah. Hamel recognized the need, but no funds were available.

The Club came back with an offer of $1,200, half of which was put up by the City of Pueblo. The City built three toilets, ten fireplaces, two shelters, and other facilities which would accommodate 125 people. The response from Puebloans was overwhelming. On an August Sunday in 1919, 700 automobiles were counted at the Squirrel Creek recreation area.

Earlier in 1919 Hamel had taken Carhart on a tour of the forest, including a view of the spectacular snowcapped Sangre de Cristo Range. Carhart was so impressed that he agreed to seriously consider recreation planning in the San Isabel National Forest.

Meanwhile, Pete Gray mentioned further recreational development to Hamel, who then made references to an association. And so it was that the Pueblo Commerce Club formed the nonprofit San Isabel Public Recreation Association (S.I.P.R.A.) on November 6, 1919. This was the first time private citizens had banded together to foster recreation development in a National Forest.

The stage was set. Carhart, who had been hired to develop a plan for the recreational use of the forests, was impressed with the beauty of the San Isabel National Forest, with the enthusiasm of Forest Supervisor Al Hamel, and with the interest of Puebloans. In addition, the S.I.P.R.A. could provide funds to put the plan into action.

During the winter of 1919–1920, Carhart wrote the plan while the Association authorized the sale of 20,000 shares of stock at $5.00 per share. Almost $6,000 was raised that winter for recreation development for the 1920 season. Carhart convinced the Association to hire Frank H. Culley, then head of the Department of Landscape Design at Iowa State College, to plan and supervise its developments. Two campgrounds were built on Squirrel Creek. Others were built on South Hardscrabble Creek and North Creek. These campgrounds may have been the first designed and built by a landscape architect in the National Forests.

During the summer of 1920, Cascade Trail at Squirrel Creek was constructed. It was designed by landscape architects to enhance the hiker's enjoyment of the natural scene, the stream, and the wildlife. The trail was for pedestrian use only, having steps and hanging bridges. It was probably the first trail specifically built in a National Forest for recreation.

The S.I.P.R.A. remained strong for several years. The construction program continued through the 1920s, adding the Ophir Creek and Davenport Campgrounds. The Boy Scout Camp Burch on South Creek and the road up Squirrel Creek to Fairview were built in 1923. The Squirrel Creek Lodge (Pueblo Municipal Building) and other structures were built about halfway up Squirrel Creek. However, by 1923 Carhart was no longer on the scene. When Congress refused to fund any expansion of recreation development in the National Forests, Carhart left the Service, realizing his dreams had been sidetracked.

With the 1929 stockmarket crash and the Depression, the activities of the S.I.P.R.A. slowed dramatically. Money was just not available. It wasn't until 1933 and the advent of the Civilian Conservation Corps (CCC) that new life would come to recreation development. The CCC would eventually take over the duties of the S.I.P.R.A.

When the S.I.P.R.A. was formed to develop recreation facilities in Squirrel Creek Canyon, the City of Pueblo, on January 15, 1920, purchased 600 acres of adjacent land to develop as Pueblo Mountain Park. The shares offered by the S.I.P.R.A. funded the construction of both park and forest facilities. As with other Carhart and S.I.P.R.A. projects, much of the work in Pueblo Mountain Park, including the trail system, was done by the CCC. The fire tower, built about 1934 or 1935, was another project. Forest conservation and fire detection were an important part of the CCC mission. In addition, fire towers were designed to provide a safe environment for recreational viewing of the surrounding mountain vistas. Walkways and platforms were built into the towers to provide rest stops as one climbed the tower.

The fire tower on West Peak in Pueblo Mountain Park certainly provides a fantastic view of the Park and the Beulah Valley. It is built with native wood and, with the exception of the replacement of a cedar shingle roof with corrugated tin, it is much the same as when it was built. A few steps have disappeared, so caution must be used if you plan to climb to the top. The tower is now braced by taut wires that run from the top four corners to the surrounding hillsides. The tower blends into the scrub oak, Douglas fir, and ponderosa pine that cover the top of the peak.

Building summer homes and cabins outside the Park was encouraged by the Forest Service in the early 1920s. It even had several blueprints or building plans that it would furnish to those who bought or leased a lot. The S.I.P.R.A. and the Forest Service advertised San Isabel National Forest through the railroads. With the enthusiasm generated by Puebloans for a mountain park at Beulah, other local communities such as Rye, Cañon City, and Florence became interested in developing their own parks.

The popularity of Pueblo Mountain Park and the Squirrel Creek Campgrounds continued for many years until the flood of 1947. In the book *From Mace's Hole, the Way It Was, to Beulah, the Way It Is,* published by the Beulah Historical Society, the caption under several photos, including one of the Squirrel Creek Lodge, says:

Snowstorms have broken communications and caused inconvenience. One of the most memorable storms began on October 31, 1946. A snowfall depth of sixty-four inches on level ground had accumulated within the next seventy-two hours. It was a widespread storm and the following June the resulting runoff of the melting snow, coupled with a two-day rain, produced a flood which washed out roadways and bridges throughout the area. It was this flood which destroyed the Squirrel Creek road, one of the most scenic drives in Colorado. The road was never reopened and the large Squirrel Creek Lodge building was left isolated and abandoned. The remains of the structure were burned in January of 1979.

It was this same flood that destroyed the Boy Scout Camp Burch on South Creek.

If you hike the Squirrel Creek Trail today, only remnants of the former activities can still be seen. Tables rot a little more each year, the sunken garbage cans are full of unemptied trash, fireplaces continue to disintegrate, and the toilets are gone. Old bridges sit beside the stream, and guardrails have collapsed along the remaining road sections. The foundation of what was once the Lodge is all that remains.

The picnic shelter, located a mile up the trail from Beulah, was restored in 1987 by the Forest Service as a testimonial to Arthur Carhart and the birth of public recreation in the National Forests. An inscription on the fireplace chimney says: "S.I.P.R.A. Sept 23, 1927." A photo in *From Mace's Hole, the Way It Was, to Beulah, the Way It Is* shows the shelter with several cars parked nearby. A photo of the original structure, built in 1919 by the Pueblo Commerce Club, is displayed on an information sign at the shelter.

Mace Legacy

Beulah was originally called Mace's Hole after Juan Mace, a Mexican outlaw and cattle rustler, who supposedly "holed" up in the area. It is said that he stole cattle and horses from local ranchers as well as from overland travelers, and kept his stolen livestock in the "Hole." If strangers came, the livestock would be driven into the lateral blind canyons. As the herds grew larger they were driven into the upper park known as the Second Mace. The livestock were later sold to ranchers along the Arkansas valley. Whether the story is fact or fiction, Juan Mace left a legacy in names—the Mace Trail in Pueblo Mountain Park and Second Mace Trail. The town was renamed Beulah in 1876.

Mining

In the late 1800s, when mining interests grew in Colorado, speculation in the Beulah area was in the higher mountains, about eight miles northwest of the valley, and received the hopeful name of Silver Circle. Although the west flank of the Wet Mountains had extensive deposits of gold and other minerals, the east flank showed no similar geologic structure, even though the Beulah area has been thoroughly prospected. One extensively developed pit is located one-half mile west of the entrance to Squirrel Creek Canyon and about a thousand feet north of the Squirrel Creek Trail. There is some hematite, galena, and chalcopyrite mineralization in the sheared part of the injection gneiss, but not in economic quantities. A second well-developed pit is located a little over two miles west of the Canyon entrance and about one-half mile north of the trail.

Mineral production in the Beulah area was limited to limestone and marble. The famous Beulah Marble, or "Beulah Red," is a rare pinkish-red marble that was used as wainscoting in the west wing of the State Capitol building in Denver. It was excavated in the 1890s from two quarries located one and one-half miles west-southwest of Beulah. The quarries were abandoned when the marble played out.

CAÑON CITY AREA

It's impossible to study the Cañon City area without getting caught up in its past and present. Railroads, railroad wars, world-class technical climbing walls, oil wells, coal fields, and dinosaurs enrich this area's heritage. A trail guide can't possibly go into depth on this interesting history and geology, but a small sampling of facts may get you to the library when the weather is too nasty to be outdoors.

North of Cañon City

North of Cañon City are Red Canyon Park and the climbing walls of Sand Gulch and The Bank. Intertwined with these are Garden Park, the Shelf Road, an oil well, and dinosaur bone discoveries.

Drive north from US 50 on Fremont County Road 9 to the first historic point (Mile 1.7 from the junction of Field Avenue and Fremont County Road 9), where there is an historic plaque marking the site of the first oil well west of the Mississippi River. Parking is inadequate, but a stop to read the marker is worthwhile. Oil once seeped from the banks of Oil Creek, now Fourmile Creek. In 1862, just across the stream, A.M. Cassidy drilled the well to a depth of 50 feet. Cassidy refined the approximately one-barrel-per-day production into kerosene and lubricating oil, which he sold in Denver for two to five dollars per gallon. This well led to the discovery in 1876, near Florence, of a larger oil field which still produces.

Continuing north to Mile 3.2 from the junction of Fremont County Road 9 and Field Avenue is the first of two monuments in the Garden Park Fossil Area. The second monument is 0.25 mile beyond. Massive bones were discovered in Garden Park in 1876 by Ormel Lucas, a local school teacher. He notified two renowned paleontologists: Othniel C. Marsh of Yale University and Edward D. Cope of the Academy of Natural Sciences in Philadelphia.

Initially Cope and Marsh were friends, but in 1869 a bitter feud began when Marsh accused Cope of attaching backwards the neck of a dinosaur. When the Cope and Marsh Quarries were opened in 1877, the "Bone Wars" began. Through their intense rivalry in the "Great Dinosaur Race" these two paleontologists would add much to our knowledge of dinosaurs.

Over about a 15-year period in the 1870s and 1880s the excavations would yield over a hundred species of dinosaurs. Apatosaurus, Diplodocus, Camarasaurus, Haplocanthosaurus, Nanosaurus, Allosaurus, Ceratosaurus, Dryosaurus, and Stegosaurus (the Colorado State Fossil) all have been found in the Garden Park Quarries. Excavations continue to yield world-class specimens. A complete stegosaurus skeleton and dinosaur eggshell fragments were discovered in 1992. Specimens extracted from the Cañon City quarries are on display at the Smithsonian Institute, the Denver Museum of Natural History, and other museums across the nation.

Continue north through Garden Park, which once grew vegetables to feed the hungry miners in Cripple Creek, to the red sandstone formations of the 500-acre Red Canyon Park. Some of the spires reach 100 feet. Another 2.75 miles north of the Park are the world-famous limestone walls of the Shelf Road Climbing Area (Sand Gulch and The Bank). These climbing walls are short but very difficult with few handholds and many overhangs.

The Shelf Road, a former stagecoach route constructed in 1892, continues to Cripple Creek. This toll road charged drivers at both ends. The lower tollkeeper's cabin can still be seen in the canyon bottom. The tollkeeper had to climb up the hill to collect the tolls each time a wagon or stagecoach passed.

The presence of dinosaurs, the sandstone of Red Canyon Park, the limestone of the climbing area, and the sandstone hogback of Skyline Drive on the west end of Cañon City speak of an inland sea. The Morrison Formation, in which dinosaur bones are found, is composed of sandstone, mudstone, siltstone, and shale, and was

The author on arch—Red Canyon Park

deposited on a vast, swampy floodplain along the edge of a retreating sea during Jurassic times, about 150 million years ago. This was a fertile, subtropical landscape with wide rivers and streams, and dinosaurs. Swamps and rivers eventually swallowed the dinosaur bones, petrifying and preserving them until the 1877 "Bone Wars" began and they were excavated.

More information and seasonal tours of the Garden Park Fossil Area can be obtained at the Dinosaur Depot at 330 Royal Gorge Boulevard (US 50) in Cañon City. Small admission and tour fees are charged.

Southwest of Cañon City

Grape Creek flows northeast from DeWeese Reservoir near Westcliffe to the Arkansas River, just west of Cañon City. If you hike the East Pierce Gulch Trail, the Temple Canyon Trail, or to The Tights, you have to cross this creek. Climbs of Tanner Peak and Curley Peak or a hike through Chute Park give nice views into a portion of the Grape Creek drainage below.

After the Royal Gorge Railroad Wars, the Denver and Rio Grande Railroad constructed many miles of track. One such track was the Grape Creek Branch, which followed Grape Creek for its entire length. When General William J. Palmer built this narrow-gauge railroad in 1881, it signaled the end of the stage and freight lines that followed the Oak Creek Grade Road from Cañon City and the Copper Gulch Road from Parkdale.

Grape Creek, however, was susceptible to floods, so the freight and stage line resumed business when the railroad track was washed out. The first washout occurred in the second year after construction, but track was rebuilt in 1884. When high water caused even greater destruction in 1889 the track was abandoned.

If you hike along Grape Creek in the Temple Canyon area the granite walls will keep you crossing the creek. The railroad made five of its 35 crossings in the Temple Canyon area. Only a few concrete structures and bent rails remain. A fun hike on a hot day, when the water is low, uses the Temple Canyon Trail to reach Grape Creek. Follow the creek upstream to where the Temple Canyon Road crosses Grape Creek and where you can leave a second vehicle. If you continue upstream from the road crossing, The Tights can be reached, mostly by following the railroad bed.

Iron Mountain, northwest of East Pierce Gulch, was developed into a source of ore for the Palmer-backed Colorado Coal and Iron Company steel mill in Pueblo. The company was later named CF&I

Steel Mill and is now known as Rocky Mountain Steel Mills. It is probable that ore was hauled to the narrow-gauge railroad at Grape Creek via West and East Pierce Gulches. Perhaps the building remnants along the creek were part of a railroad siding.

RYE AREA

At 12,347' Greenhorn Mountain is the tallest peak in the Wet Mountain Range, which extends from Cañon City on the north to Badito on the south. The range was formed when a fault uplifted the Precambrian granite and metamorphic rocks and thrust them eastward onto younger sedimentary layers. Rain and snow-laden clouds often hide the range from the plains below. The Indians, the Spanish, and a party of early Morman emigrants all named the range "Wet Mountains."

Greenhorn Mountain is part of the 22,040-acre Greenhorn Mountain Wilderness Area. Greenhorn, or Cuerno Verde in Spanish, recalls the Comanche Chief Cuerno Verde, who was killed in 1779 on the plains below the peak in a fierce battle with Spanish soldiers led by Juan Bautista de Anza, the Governor of New Mexico.

SAN ISABEL AREA
Lake Isabel

Lake Isabel, one of the most popular recreation areas in the Wet Mountains, is surrounded by trailheads for the Snowslide, Cisneros, Marion Mine, and Saint Charles Trails.

One of the last projects of the San Isabel Public Recreation Association (see "Beulah Area" history) was to purchase land to build a large dam, lake, and campground. The dam would be built by the Civilian Conservation Corps (CCC). Construction started in 1935. Filling of the lake began in the spring of 1938 and a lodge was opened to the public that summer. The dam was completed in the spring of 1939, and the new lake immediately became the most popular recreation water in Southern Colorado. On July 4, 1939, a reporter counted 490 autos at what came to be known as Lake Isabel.

Marion Mine and Lake

Three miles west of Lake Isabel on Amethyst Creek are the ruins of the Marion Mine. Zina H. Fairchild discovered the first quartz in 1880 and filed a claim in Custer County in 1881. On March 23, 1885, Fairchild sold half interest in his claim to S. Wixon and James Graves for $1,000. Work on the tunnel was started, and in that same year the prospectors found a vein of ore containing zinc, galena, copper, a few ounces of silver, and close to $1 in gold per ton. The three partners were unable to make a profit, so they sold the claim to Frank Buckley, Henry E. and Marion McElwain, and Henry G. Gray for $20,000 in 1906. Mine headquarters were in Denver.

Originally known as Fairchild's property, with a post office address at Fairview, the mine was renamed Marion, after McElwain's wife. The Marion Mine began operating in 1907 and consisted of a four-story mill building, office, boarding house, and other dwellings. Two other mines—the Sam Davis, located a half mile west of the mill, and the Dewey, a mile south of the mill—were also part of the property. Pack burros and mules were used to transport the ore from these mines to the mill at Marion Mine.

The mill was 150 feet from the Marion Mine entrance. The ore cars, pushed by hand from the tunnel entrance to the mill, were emptied into a large crusher at the top of the mill. Processing the ore consisted of moving it from the crusher to six large rolls, through revolving screens, the tube mill, finer revolving screens, the flotation machine, and finally, the concentration table. These processes pulverized the ore and removed waste before the ore was put into strong canvas sacks.

Ore was shipped in wagons pulled by four horses to a railroad siding at Graneros, east of Rye. The 60-mile round trip took four days. The railroad then transported the ore to a Florence smeltery. The reduction mills in Florence were also processing gold ore brought through Phantom Canyon from Cripple Creek.

Water was used to provide a cost-effective power source for the mill. In the early 1900s, snowfall was about 30 feet each season. The spring runoff and summer rain showers provided an ample water supply. A swampy flat, 1.25 miles northwest of the mill and 1,100 feet higher than the mill, provided an ideal place for the reservoir that came to be known as Marion Lake. A log cribbing dam, filled with granite blasted from the adjoining hills, was constructed between two rocky points that were 350 feet apart. The dam, 45 feet high, had a capacity of about 30,000,000 cubic feet of water and backed water for about a mile. A ten-inch pipeline brought the water down to the mill, where the pipe was then reduced to three-quarter-inch, giving pressure of 465 pounds per square inch. The main waterwheel developed 500 horsepower.

Besides running the ore processing machinery, the water power was used to produce electricity for the mill and other buildings in the mine complex. There was a compressor to run the drilling machines in the mine, a complete assay office, a blacksmith shop, and a large boiler for heat in the mill.

A steam engine at the reservoir powered a sawmill that provided the planks for the dam, the mine timbers, and the lumber for the mill and other mine buildings. About 80 men worked during the building of the reservoir, some in the sawmill and others in the dam construction.

Horse and wagon hauled all the machinery to the mine. Some of the machinery was so heavy, eight or ten horses were required to pull a wagon up the very steep road, carrying a single part of a machine.

During the winter, temperatures would drop to 30 or 35 degrees below zero and the reservoir would freeze. The mine was located in a deep canyon with only three hours of sun per day in winter. The deep snow made it almost impossible to get to Rye, so the mill would shut down until spring.

George Kindle was the mining engineer from 1908 until the mine closed in 1915. He remained the caretaker until 1933. His wife, Hattie, ran the boarding house at the mine and cooked for 20 miners. She baked all the bread for the men at the reservoir and the boarders at the mine. Their son, Henry F. Kindle, lived at the mine from age one month to about 22 years of age. He later became a Pueblo resident.

When the mine finally closed, between 4,500 and 5,000 feet of tunnel had been built and about 200,000 tons of ore had been removed.

TRAIL DESCRIPTIONS

BEULAH AREA

PUEBLO MOUNTAIN PARK TRAILS

General description: Features a railed overlook, a fire tower, the ruins of an old camp, ridges, canyons, and good views on a pleasant variety of trails.

Elevations in park: Highest: 7,400' Lowest: 6,680'

Miles in park: 6

Rating: Easy

USGS topo map: Saint Charles Peak

Users: Foot or horse traffic only

Overview and road directions: There are two trailhead areas in Pueblo Mountain Park linked by an 0.8-mile upper scenic road. The trailheads for **Mace, Lookout Point, Devil's Canyon,** and **North Ridge Trails** are at the north end of the park. **Tower Trail** and **South Creek Trail** are at the south end of the park. The **Camp Burch and Ranger Trail** is accessed from Mace Trail, Tower Trail, or South Creek Trail. Because the 6.0 miles of park trails are linked to each other, primarily by the Mace Trail, there is a variety of options in selecting a route that fits your physical condition and desired hiking time. Refer to the map on page 29 for the relationships of these trails.

To reach the main park entrance, drive 2.7 miles west on CO 78 from the main ("Y") turnoff to Beulah. Unless you are familiar with the park, avoid using the lower entrance on Mountain Park Road, which is 0.4 mile before the main entrance.

From the main park entrance follow the signs to the Ball Park for trails at the north end. The trailhead is 0.2 mile beyond (north of) the Ball Park at the hairpin turn in the road, but the best parking is 0.1 mile north of the Ball Park. From the north trailhead the road continues south on the upper scenic road to the south trailhead.

From the main park entrance the trails at the south end of the park can be reached by following the "Scenic Highway/Trails" signs. Just beyond the basketball court, take the right fork where the sign is missing. When you reach the Tower Trail sign at a "T" intersection, note that the road to the right (north) is the upper scenic road and

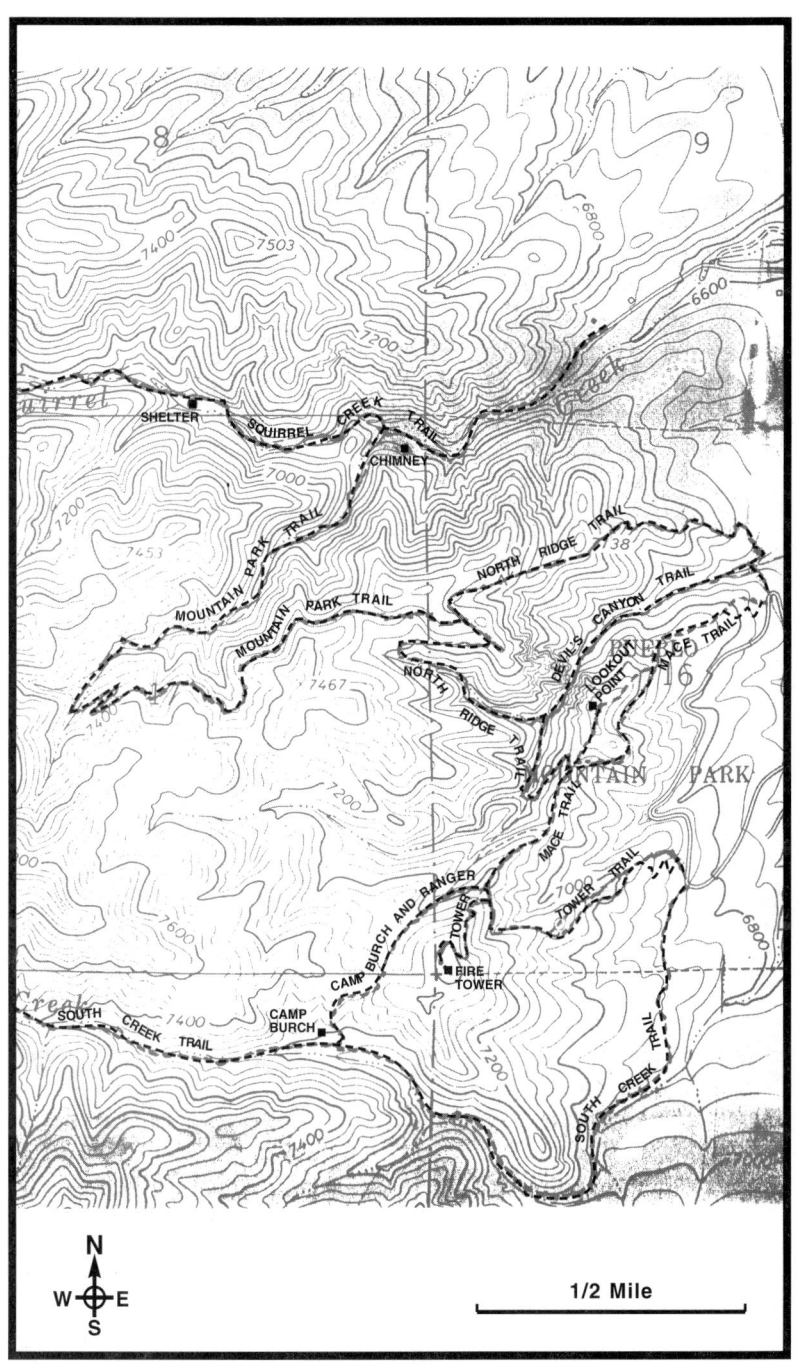

leads to the trailhead at the north end of the park. Turn left (south) at the "T" intersection to reach a parking area in 0.1 mile for Tower Trail and South Creek Trail. The cable across the road at the parking area marks the trail head for the South Creek Trail. You must ask permission to cross this lower eastern section of the South Creek Trail. It is best to use the Tower Trail, and Camp Burch and Ranger Trail to reach the South Creek Trail at Camp Burch. For the Tower Trail, hike the 0.1 mile up the road to the "T" intersection and the sign to reach the trailhead.

MACE TRAIL AND LOOKOUT POINT TRAIL

Option #1: *Elevation gain, Mace Trail to fire tower with side trip to Lookout Point:* 760'

    Elevations: Highest: 7,400'   Lowest: 6,720'

    Miles (round trip): 2.7

Option #2: *Elevation gain, Mace and Tower Trails, including side trip to the tower (with car shuttle):* 760'

    Elevations: Highest: 7,400'   Lowest: 6,720'

    Miles (one way): 2.25

Don't confuse the Mace Trail with the Second Mace Trail. The **Mace Trail** ties one end of the Pueblo Mountain Park trail system to the other end and gives flexibility in doing loop trips and side trips (see appropriate description).

The trailhead is just a few yards south of the North Ridge and Devil's Canyon trailhead. The trail begins up the steps, turns south, and gains the ridge via a few switchbacks. After 0.6 mile the trail forks at a signpost. The trail to the right (northeast) is the **Lookout Point Trail** and leads to Lookout Point in 0.1 mile. There is a platform, built in 1934, with a pipe safety railing which should keep you from falling as you peer down into Devil's Canyon.

Retrace your steps to the Mace Trail. Just a few feet farther south on the Mace Trail is the junction with the North Ridge Trail. After another quarter mile southwest along the ridge, the Mace Trail comes to the junction with the Camp Burch and Ranger Trail. A few feet beyond this junction is the Tower Trail, where the Mace Trail ends.

Lookout Point at Devil's Canyon—Lookout Point Trail

Proceed down the Tower Trail to the trailhead parking at the south end of the park. If you're not doing a car shuttle and your car is 0.1 mile north of the Ball Park, it is 1.0 mile back to your car via the upper scenic road, or 0.75 mile if you follow the signs through the middle of the park to the Ball Park.

NORTH RIDGE TRAIL AND DEVIL'S CANYON TRAIL

Option #1: *Elevation gain, North Ridge and Devil's Canyon Trails loop:* 600'

   Elevations: Highest: 7,280'   Lowest: 6,680'

   Miles (for loop): 2

Option #2: *Elevation gain, North Ridge and Mace Trails loop (with Devil's Canyon side trip):* 750'

   Elevations: Highest: 7,280'   Lowest: 6,680'

   Miles (for loop with side trip): 3.1

The **North Ridge** and **Devil's Canyon Trails** make a nice loop trip if the water is not too high in Devil's Canyon. Or use the North Ridge and Mace Trails to make a slightly larger loop with Devil's Canyon explored as a side trip.

From the trailhead, the North Ridge and Devil's Canyon Trails head north, downhill, for 0.1 mile to the Devil's Canyon creek bed. Cross the creek bed and hike up the steps to an old road and a sign. The road to the left (southwest) leads to Devil's Canyon (a dead end according to the sign), while the road to the right (northeast) goes to the North Ridge Trail.

Devil's Canyon is a dead end only if a short icefall in the winter or high water in warmer weather cause the less adventurous to retrace their steps. As you begin your hike into Devil's Canyon, note the few scars on the hillside and a steel elevated gravity loading frame with sizing screen that are now the only evidence of a quarry that once supplied stone for the park's bridges, drainage projects, and the first caretaker's house. Rock was last quarried in the 1970s. The Devil's Canyon Trail crosses the creek bed several times to reach the falls. The canyon walls, highly folded and faulted, are essentially batholithic granite of the Mesozoic Era. Regardless of your hiking abilities, the 0.3-mile hike into Devil's Canyon is worth the effort. If you continue through the canyon beyond the falls, the trail will intersect the southern end of the North Ridge Trail.

Retrace your steps out of Devil's Canyon in high water or icy conditions to hike the North Ridge Trail. From the sign at the Devil's Canyon/North Ridge Trails junction on the road, follow the road (northeast) the few yards to the corner of a hayfield, where the trail turns north and leaves the road. The hayfield once grew hay for the City Park Zoo in Pueblo. As the North Ridge Trail works its way up the hillside there are nice views into Devil's Canyon. At the top of the hill 1.0 mile from the trailhead the trail intersects with Mountain Park Trail #1385 (right fork), which descends to Squirrel Creek Trail #1384 in 1.3 miles (see "Squirrel Creek Trail" section). From the North Ridge and Mountain Park Trails junction it is 0.1 mile to the San Isabel National Forest boundary on the Mountain Park Trail.

Continuing southeast on the North Ridge Trail, a short side trail to the left leads to a ridge overlooking Devil's Canyon. Take a few minutes to explore and enjoy the area before beginning your descent.

After leaving the overlook the trail heads northwest a few feet, then goes west to a gully. At the gully the trail turns south and descends to an intermittent creek bed. The trail stays on the left (north) side of the creek bed until the canyon narrows and a second gully comes in from the right. The trail crosses at this point to the south side of the creek bed where it remains through the narrow canyon. Exiting the canyon, it crosses back to the north side of the creek and intersects with the southwest end of Devil's Canyon Trail coming from the left (north). The North Ridge Trail continues to the right (south) to its junction with the Mace Trail.

If you turn left (north) at this junction to hike through Devil's Canyon, you will find yourself at the bottom of the rock wall that only minutes before you were exploring from above. Steep trails, requiring a bit of scrambling, lead out of the canyon bottom to the North Ridge Trail overlook (west) or to Lookout Point (east). These are not official park trails, but their usage has not been controlled. Continuing northeast out of the canyon you'll need to negotiate the short waterfall (icefall) that may make the Devil's Canyon Trail a dead end, then cross the stream bed several times before returning to the junction with the North Ridge Trail.

If, instead of hiking northeast through Devil's Canyon, you've decided to continue south on the North Ridge Trail to its junction with the Mace Trail, note the gully to the southwest where the trail crosses the creek and turns northeast. The trail at one time continued up this gully, but now switchbacks up the hillside. Note the post with arrow sign to keep you from hiking up the gully. Hike northeast from the creek bed to the next switchback (about 0.1 mile) which changes the trail direction to southwest, and in a few yards you will encounter a junction. Do not go right at this junction as it will take you back to the bottom of the gully and the arrow sign for the closed trail at the creek crossing. Instead, go left at this junction to join the Mace Trail just a few feet south of the trail to Lookout Point. The Mace Trail can be followed northeast (left) back to your car (see "Mace Trail and Lookout Point Trail" section).

TOWER TRAIL

Elevation gain: 560'

Elevations: Highest: 7,400' Lowest: 6,840'

Miles (round trip): 2

The **Tower Trail** heads north from the trailhead sign but quickly begins a series of switchbacks to gain the ridge in 0.2 mile. After another 0.5 mile watch for an intersection and trail sign where a trail

Fire tower—Tower Trail

to the left is a continuation of the Tower Trail. The trail straight ahead from this intersection is the south end of the Mace Trail. If you reach the sign for Camp Burch and Ranger Trail, Fire Tower, Lookout Point/Mace, and North Ridge Trails, you have passed the continuation of the Tower Trail by a few feet. Retrace your steps to continue the Tower Trail. Start up the hill for a few feet until you reach the switchback trail, which takes you in 0.3 mile to the fire tower.

The tower, built in the mid-1930s, offers great views of the surrounding hillsides. Climb the tower at your own risk. As with any manmade structure, time can cause deterioration, so examine the tower carefully before you scramble to the top. It's also a good place for lunch if you plan to retrace your steps to the car.

CAMP BURCH AND RANGER TRAIL

Elevation gain for Tower, and Camp Burch and Ranger Trails to Camp Burch, with side trip to tower: 840'

Miles (round trip): 3

The **Camp Burch and Ranger Trail** is a 0.5-mile-long connecting trail that begins at the south end of the Mace Trail (see "Mace Trail" section) and ends in the San Isabel National Forest on the South Creek Trail at remnants of the Boy Scouts' Camp Burch (see "South Creek Trail" section). It can also be reached by hiking the Tower Trail (see "Tower Trail" section). From the junction with the Mace Trail, the Camp Burch and Ranger Trail takes you over a ridge, then descends to the camp, which was destroyed in the 1947 flood. Take a few moments to explore the ruins before retracing your steps.

SOUTH CREEK TRAIL #1321

General description: A pleasant mountain trail with Camp Burch ruins to add an historic touch.

Elevation loss: 2,760'

Elevation gain if staying on South Creek Trail through private property: 500'

Elevations: Highest: 9,600' Lowest: 6,840'

Miles (one way): 7.25

Rating: Moderate

USGS topo map: Saint Charles Peak

Users: Horses, hikers

Road directions: The east end of the South Creek Trail is at the south end of Pueblo Mountain Park (see "Pueblo Mountain Park Trails—Overview and road directions" section). The west end is on CO 165. The entire trail is best done as a car shuttle beginning at CO 165. From San Isabel drive north on CO 165 over Greenhill Divide (3.2 miles) to the trailhead at 3.9 miles from San Isabel (Forest Road 327). There is a trailhead sign 0.2 mile before the trailhead. If you reach the Saint Charles Peak trailhead you are 0.1 mile too far.

There is parking for one car at the highway at the top of Forest Road 327. Shoulder parking along the highway is also an option, as well as using the Saint Charles Peak trailhead parking area. If you have a high-clearance vehicle, drive down Forest Road 327 (0.05 mile) to the grassy parking area.

South Creek Trail begins at 9,100' in what is known as Lion Park (refer to a topographic map). The trail heads east-southeast down the road (you will lose some elevation) to a junction. Go right at the junction, continuing to a large parking area (Mile 0.15 from CO 165). If you've driven to this point, do not drive farther, as turn-around areas are limited. The road crosses a culvert, turns northeast for a few yards, then turns southeast. At Mile 0.4 from CO 165, leave the road at a South Creek Trail sign and cross the creek to continue the South Creek Trail. The trail now climbs to 9,600' in 0.5 mile before it begins its descent to Pueblo Mountain Park at 6,840'. At Mile 4 there is a cutover trail to the left (north) which leads to the Squirrel Creek Trail. This 0.5-mile-long cutover trail lends more options for trips.

Continue another 2.0 miles east along the South Creek Trail to the remnants of the Boy Scouts' Camp Burch and a trail junction. The left fork is the Camp Burch and Ranger Trail, which leads to the Mace and Tower Trails in Pueblo Mountain Park. This is the preferred route to complete the trip because of the private property along the lower end of the South Creek Trail. There will be a 160' elevation gain if you follow this route. The right fork is the old Camp Burch Road, now the South Creek Trail. You **must** have permission to cross the private property. This road/trail follows the creek southeast and enters the private property before turning north and continuing to the trailhead parking at the south end of Pueblo Mountain Park. The east end of the trail requires climbing over a metal gate 100 yards before reaching the parking area. Step over or walk around either end of the cable that blocks the road/trail at the parking area.

Note that the section of South Creek Trail between Camp Burch and the Pueblo Mountain Park trailhead does not cross South Creek. A couple of side roads may tempt you, but they cross the creek. Remember to close the gate at the forest/private property boundary. Please respect private property.

SQUIRREL CREEK TRAIL #1384

General description: A delightful trail when the water is low, with many remnants from days when there was a road along Squirrel Creek.

Elevation gain: 1,800'

Elevations: Highest: 8,450'   Lowest: 6,650'

Miles (round trip on maintained trail):   10.5

Rating: Moderate

USGS topo map: Saint Charles Peak

Users: Horses, mountain bikers, hikers, backpackers (no permit required)

Road directions: Squirrel Creek Trail has its east end in Beulah. The west end is at Davenport Campground off CO 165. For the Beulah trailhead take CO 78 from Pueblo to the "Y" (junction CO 78 West and CO 78 Business) in Beulah. At the "Y" go left for 1.4 miles on CO 78 West (toward Pueblo Mountain Park and CO 165) to Squirrel Creek Road, which continues straight ahead (west) while CO 78 West makes a sharp bend to the left (south). Squirrel Creek Road immediately crosses the bridge over South Creek. A right fork after the South Creek bridge crossing is Pennsylvania Avenue and leads to the main street in Beulah. Follow Squirrel Creek Road straight ahead (west) for 1.3 miles until it dead-ends at an iron gate and the trailhead. A walk-through access on the right side of the gate has

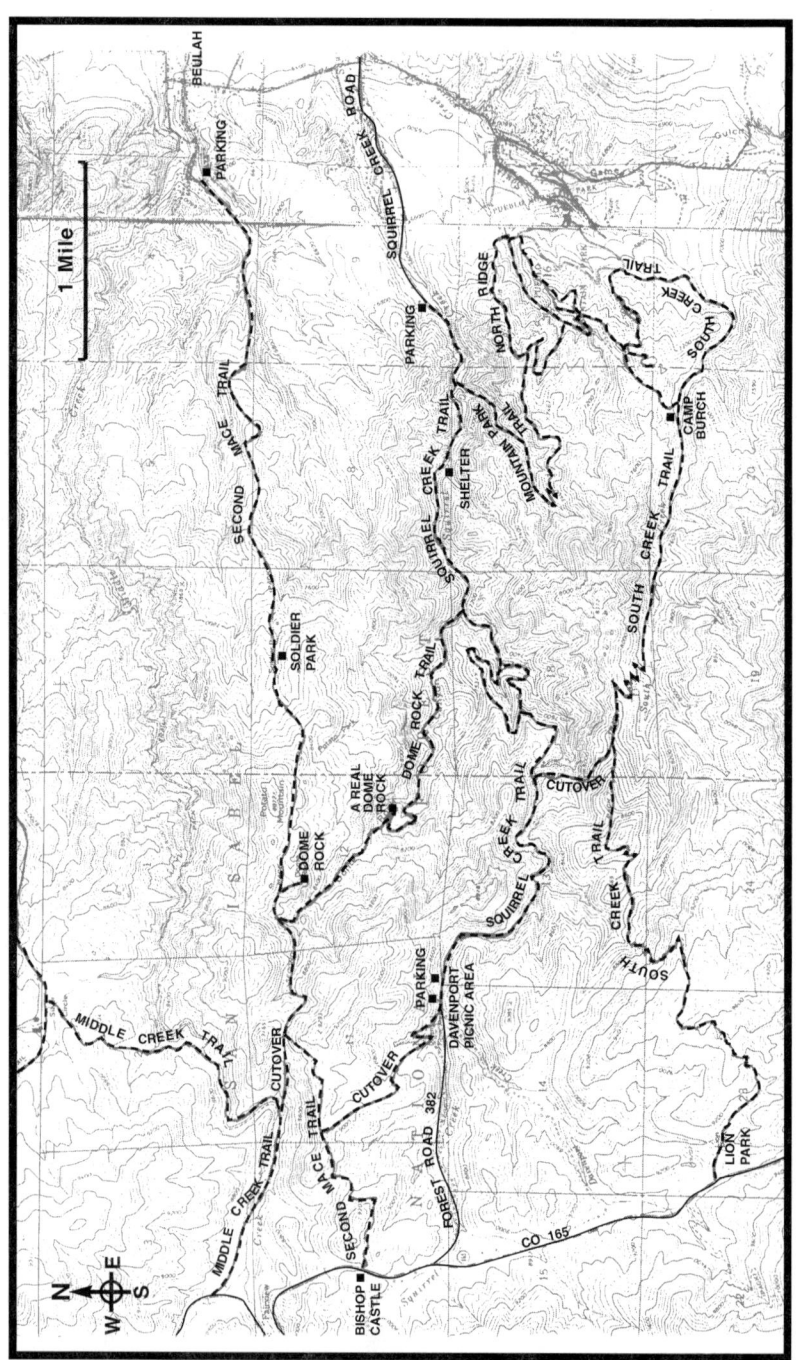

been provided. Park along the side of the road, being careful not to block private driveways and gates. Please respect private property.

To reach the trailhead in Davenport Campground, drive 5.3 miles north of San Isabel on CO 165 to the campground entrance (Forest Road 382). Drive 1.5 miles to the end of the campground road and park in the small parking area at the trailhead.

The **Squirrel Creek Trail** from the Beulah trailhead reaches the National Forest boundary in 0.3 mile with one crossing of Squirrel Creek. To reach the boundary, hike southwest on the road, staying on the north side of Squirrel Creek. In 0.2 mile from the trailhead watch for a Forest Service sign on the left side of the road. At the sign, leave the road (which switchbacks up the hillside) and follow the trail (downhill and west), which immediately crosses Squirrel Creek. After another 0.1 mile is the forest boundary sign. Just past the boundary sign is an old chimney, a remnant of another day.

At Mile 0.5 from the trailhead the trail comes to a junction with Mountain Park Trail #1385 (straight ahead), which leads to the Pueblo Mountain Park boundary in 1.2 miles and the Mountain Park trailhead (Devil's Canyon/North Ridge trailhead) in 2.3 miles (see "North Ridge Trail/Devil's Canyon Trail" description). To the right is Squirrel Creek Trail #1384 to Davenport Campground, 3.9 miles away.

At this junction the trail again crosses Squirrel Creek. But don't settle into having successfully negotiated the creek crossing, as you will cross it 32 more times before getting to the campground. Except in high water runoff, crossings have big, dry, and usually stable stepping stones. Use care to avoid a dunking. Look in the deep pools for fish!

A half dozen more obvious creek crossings and a half mile from the Squirrel Creek Trail and Mountain Park Trail junction is a picnic shelter that was restored in 1987. It's a great place for lunch, and a welcome sight in a sudden rain shower. There are picnic tables along the next 0.75 mile that are in various states of disrepair, but usable. At the end of this 0.75 mile, Squirrel Creek Trail intersects with the Dome Rock Trail (right fork), which is a cutover trail to the Second Mace Trail.

Continuing left on the Squirrel Creek Trail for another 0.5 mile brings you to more picnic tables. At a very nice table with a bricked fireplace nearby, the trail turns sharply to the north, away from the creek. A few feet after the turn an unmarked trail comes in from the left. This is a shortcut trail shown on topo maps that can be difficult to follow. The maintained trail from this point follows a section of the old road not washed out in the 1947 flood. After a mile on the maintained trail (road) the shortcut trail rejoins it.

If you've chosen to stay on the maintained trail, after going north, then west for 0.1 mile, the trail turns northeast for 0.25 mile before turning southwest for 0.5 mile, and finally east for 0.1 mile, where it rejoins the shortcut trail and turns south.

If you have some trail-finding experience you may wish to take the shortcut trail because it saves a half mile one way. If your experience is limited, the trail is easier to follow going down, if you wish to explore it on the return trip. For those wishing to attempt it, a signless post is encountered just a few feet up the shortcut trail. Then several fallen trees must be circumvented. At 0.1 mile beyond the signless post, a fairly large tree has fallen across the trail. Clamber over or hike around the end of this tree. The trail here becomes overgrown but can be followed to what looks like a trail junction. At this junction the trail seems to continue straight ahead as a road but is blocked off by another tree; this is **not** the trail. At this seeming junction the real trail turns north (right), then quickly switches southwest and disappears again at a grass-covered washout. Hike around the washout to the left. From above the washout both ends of

Picnic shelter—Squirrel Creek Trail

the trail are visible. From the top of the washout the trail heads north (to the right). In 0.1 mile it will again switch southwest. The next obscure area is 0.25 mile farther. Below a steep embankment to the right, the shortcut trail becomes roadlike and is again blocked by trees. A path up the steep embankment leads to the maintained trail (the old road). From the junction of the shortcut trail and the maintained trail, turn left (south) to continue to Davenport Campground.

Before leaving the junction of the shortcut trail and the maintained trail, note the old concrete structures which once were part of a guardrail. From this junction another 0.5 mile brings you to a foundation, the remnants of the old Squirrel Creek Lodge. This is a nice camping area. Just beyond the Lodge watch for an obscure and somewhat overgrown trail to the left, marked by a cairn. The obscure trail crossing the creek is a 0.5-mile-long cutover trail to the South Creek Trail. The Squirrel Creek Trail continues straight ahead from this junction for another 1.5 miles and eight creek crossings, bringing you to the Davenport Campground.

Top: *Squirrel Creek Lodge in its early days*
(Photo by M/M Roy Simonson, courtesy of Beulah Historical Society)
Bottom: *Squirrel Creek Lodge today—Squirrel Creek Trail*

SECOND MACE TRAIL #1322

General description: From Beulah the trail has nice views of the Beulah Valley and Pueblo Mountain Park, but it can be steep and permission is needed to cross private property.

Elevation gain to CO 165: 2,820'

Elevations: Highest to CO 165: 9,200'   Lowest: 6,500'

Miles (one way including road section at east end):   6.75

Rating: Moderate

USGS topo maps: Beulah, Saint Charles Peak

Users: Hikers

Road directions (Beulah): The Second Mace Trail's east end begins in Beulah and the west end on CO 165 south of Fairview at the Bishop Castle (see "Ophir Creek—Bigelow Divide Area: Second Mace Trail" section). It's best to hike from CO 165 and return to that point because of the private property in Beulah. Current property owners are allowing access at Beulah but any abuse or misuse of this privilege could close the trail at the lower (east) end. If you do hike from Beulah get permission from the landowner first (see trail description) and limit the number of hikers to eight or less. No one wants 20 people hiking through their front yard.

Finding the trailhead in Beulah is a bit of a challenge. Follow your topo maps closely until you're definitely on the trail. Drive west through Beulah on Grand Avenue, beyond the U-turn to the junction of Pine Avenue (not Pine Drive) and Cascade Avenue. Turn right onto Cascade Avenue for 0.2 mile to its intersection with Vine Mesa Avenue. Turn left onto Vine Mesa Avenue for 0.1 mile and park your car along the road (room for two cars) outside the gate. You may need to climb over the gate to begin the hike.

Start the hike of **Second Mace Trail** by heading southwest on the road 0.3 mile to a junction. The left fork crosses a creek bed—**do not go that way**. Take the right fork (straight ahead) which within a few feet makes a 90-degree turn and reaches an A-frame-style house. Prior to beginning your hike, you should have contacted the owner of this house to get permission to cross his property. Hike up the hill toward the house until you reach the opening in the electric fence opposite the detached garage. Go through the fence opening (left) and hike southwest along the hillside on what appears to have previously been a graded road. A trail drops off the end of this graded section onto another road. If you're making a round trip, remember to go back up this short trail so you can get through the electric fence without wandering all over the meadow it encloses.

Continue to the right from this junction to a locked metal gate that partially blocks the road. On the left side of the metal gate is a barbed wire gate that you'll need to go through. Please close the gate behind you if it was closed. Just beyond the gate and the barbed wire fence line, the trail (road) comes to a drainage and a small clearing. Completely cross the drainage to the left, going over an old culvert that is in the middle of the drainage. A trail and the drainage lie on either side of a large ponderosa pine tree. Ignore both trails and continue to the left side of a smaller ponderosa pine tree growing in the middle of the meadow.

At the smaller ponderosa pine tree two trails can be seen. An obvious trail heads northwest while a wide but overgrown path leads due west. Take the overgrown trail that leads west. It quickly becomes a good but sometimes steep trail, complete with a post trail marker and some very old blazes. Years of motorcycles on the trail have worn it three feet deep in places and left scratch marks on the rocks. Motorcyclists now rarely use the east end of this trail.

From the A-frame house, the trail crosses private property for 0.75 mile. Please stay on the trail.

At Mile 3.25 from where you parked your car is Soldier Park. This delightful meadow has no long-range views, but there are two huge white fir trees at the west edge of the meadow that are growing so close together, it's difficult to tell if they come from one base or two. A dead tree is squeezed between the two firs. Soldier Park is a nice destination for a short round-trip hike.

DOME ROCK TRAIL #1387

General description: A cutover trail that allows a loop trip to be made using Second Mace and Squirrel Creek Trails.

Elevation gain (loop from Davenport Campground): 1,960'

Elevations: Highest: 9,080'   Lowest: 7,120'

Miles (round trip): 8.5

Rating: Moderate for loop

USGS topo map: Saint Charles Peak

Users: Hikers

Dome Rock Trail is a cutover trail between Squirrel Creek and Second Mace Trails. The Squirrel Creek/Dome Rock Trail junction is 1.75 miles from the Squirrel Creek trailhead in Beulah or 3.5 miles from the Davenport Campground trailhead. The Second Mace Trail/Dome Rock Trail junction is 2.25 miles from CO 165 or 4.5 miles from the Vine Mesa Avenue parking in Beulah.

The Dome Rock Trail is 2.5 miles in length. If a car is left at Davenport Campground at the Squirrel Creek trailhead and a car at the Second Mace trailhead on CO 165, an 8.25-mile loop trip can be made using the Dome Rock Trail. Or with one car use the Second Mace Cutover Trail from Davenport Campground to hike an 8.5-mile loop. Dome Rock Trail, like the Squirrel Creek Trail, has many creek crossings, but the creek is small and usually dry (see "Second Mace Trail" and "Squirrel Creek Trail" descriptions).

If you wish to scramble to the top of Dome Rock that is marked on the topographic map, hike east on the Second Mace Trail for about 0.1 mile from the junction of Dome Rock and Second Mace Trails. Bushwhack south from Second Mace Trail to the top of Dome Rock. This is actually not a very interesting place. A much more interesting real dome rock is along the Dome Rock Trail. The rock is 1.0 mile down the Dome Rock Trail from the Second Mace Trail or 1.5 miles up from the Squirrel Creek Trail.

CAÑON CITY AREA

ARKANSAS RIVERWALK—CAÑON CITY

General description: A riparian area along the south bank of the Arkansas River in the heart of Cañon City which offers fishing and wildlife viewing.

Elevation gain: None

Elevation: 5,300'

Miles (round trip): 5.5

Rating: Easy

Maps: Cañon City (USGS quad),
www.coloradolottery.com/about/trailmaps

Users: Horses (except on the River Trail), hikers, bikers

Road directions: This 2.75-mile easy unpaved riparian-area trail runs along the south bank of the Arkansas River in Cañon City between MacKenzie Avenue on the east and John Griffin Regional Park on the west. Access and parking are reached on the east by driving south from US 50 on MacKenzie Avenue for 2.0 miles to Santa Fe Drive. Turn west onto Santa Fe Drive. The parking area is 0.4 mile. Access on the west end is from CO 115 (9th Street). From the junction of CO 115 and US 50 drive 0.3 mile south on CO 115, then turn east onto Sell Avenue, the road immediately after crossing the railroad tracks. This leads to a parking area in 0.4 mile. A third access, with parking, is available by following the Gold Belt Tour—Scenic Byway signs in east Cañon City, at the junction of US 50 and South Raynolds Avenue, south 1.0 mile to the Arkansas Riverwalk parking area on Ash Street (the street name changes to Ash Street at the bridge). Pets must be on a leash.

The **Arkansas Riverwalk** follows a former railroad right-of-way. The east end of the trail, called Brookside Junction Trail, runs 1.5 miles between the parking at MacKenzie Avenue and the parking at the Raynolds Bridge Trailhead. About a mile of the Brookside Junction Trail is squeezed between the Arkansas River and the bluffs.

The west end of the trail forms a loop around John Griffin Regional Park, which is between the Raynolds Bridge Trailhead parking and the 9th Street parking. The southern section of the loop is the Bluff Trail and the riverside section is the River Trail. Each is 1.0 mile long. An old road with access to the River Trail and Bluff Trail runs through the middle of John Griffin Regional Park, so your route can take many different forms. The main trails are marked every quarter mile. A trail has been built under Raynolds Bridge so that you do not have to cross this busy road unless you are on a horse riding the Brookside Junction Trail and the Bluff Trail.

Benches, picnic tables, and vault toilets are plentiful. Fishing and wildlife viewing areas are available. This popular trail will hopefully be extended in the near future.

FREMONT PEAK

General description: An easy climb at the west edge of Cañon City with some great views of the surrounding countryside.

Elevation gain: 515' to Fremont Peak, 950' with extra 0.5 mile

Elevations: Highest: 7,233' Lowest: 6,784'

Miles (round trip to top of peak only): 3.5

Rating: Easy

USGS topo map: Royal Gorge (7.5')

Users: Hikers

Road directions: From the west end of Cañon City (junction First Street/US 50 at Veterans Park) drive 7.7 miles west on US 50 to the east entrance of the Royal Gorge Park. Turn south (left) onto the park access road (Fremont County Road 3-A) and drive 2.7 miles to the park boundary (no toll booth). Go up the hill a half mile, watching for a picnic area on the left (east), at the top of the hill. Drive 0.1 mile beyond the picnic ground entrance and turn left onto what is actually the middle of three access roads to the Fremont Peak area. Follow this dirt road east for 0.7 mile, then take the right fork into the picnic and campground area. The first road to the right (0.1 mile) in the picnic/campground area leads to Fremont Peak. Park your vehicle near this junction. Parking may be limited if there are many picnickers and campers. Don't be tempted to drive up the road toward Fremont Peak for parking because a sign at the bottom of the hill says "No vehicles beyond this point," and a locked gate 0.1 mile from the junction will keep you from driving where you don't belong.

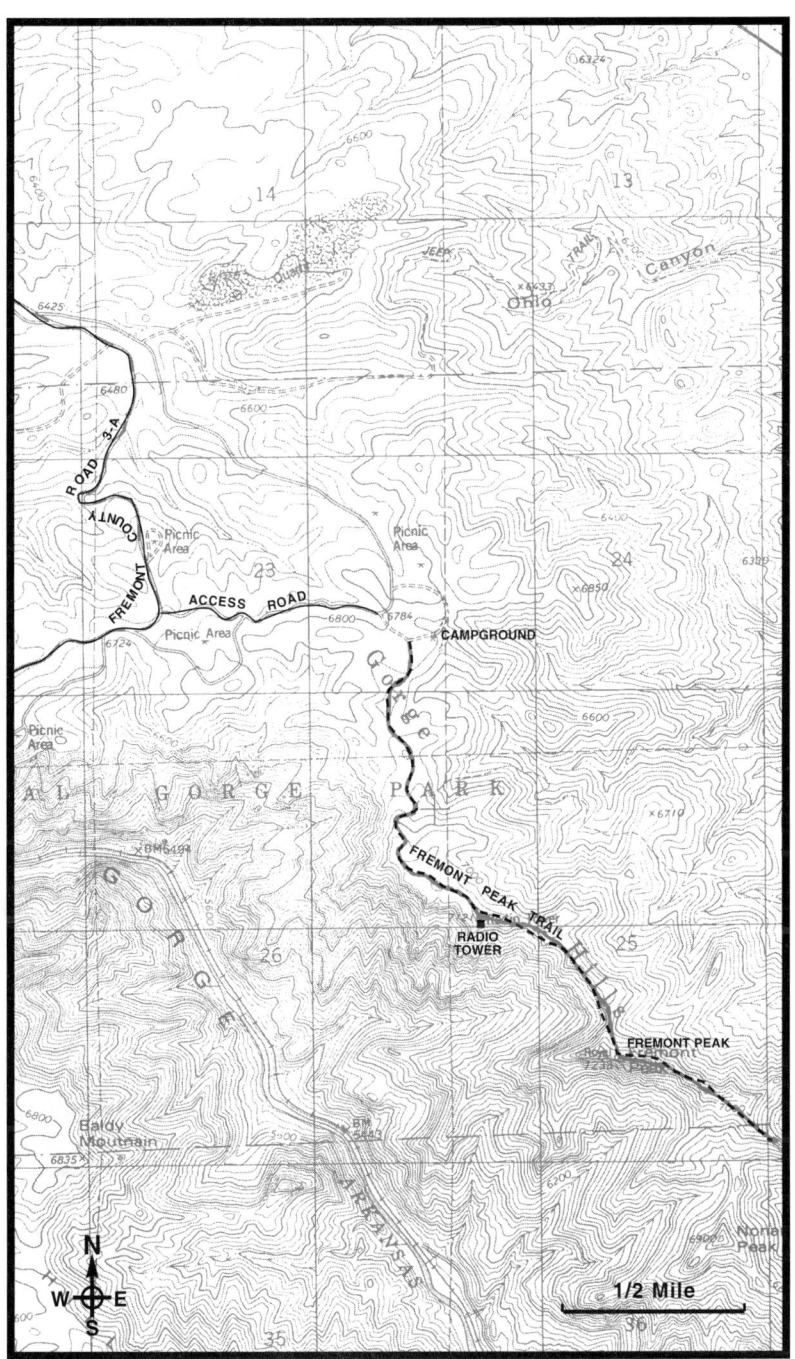

The hike to **Fremont Peak** follows the road heading south and southeast, coming first to a building and then to the radio tower. There is a great view of the Arkansas River and the Royal Gorge Canyon along this road. Other nice views are of Cañon City, the campground, the Buckskin Joe area, Pikes Peak, and the Sangre de Cristo Mountains.

The road from the building to the radio tower is overgrown but can be followed without too much difficulty. The road continues from the building to the radio tower on the north side of the power lines. You will lose several feet in elevation between the building and the radio tower as the ridge drops to a saddle.

Beyond the radio tower sturdy hiking shoes are recommended to protect the feet and ankles from cactus. The trail continues from the corner of the radio tower fence under the power lines, which head east toward Cañon City. Again you will lose a bit of elevation under the power lines.

The trail becomes overgrown, but if you stay close to the ridge top, trail sections can be found and followed. Be careful of the cholla, prickly pear cactus, and yucca. The trail makes yet another downhill dip. After the third dip, when you need the trail the most to reach the top, it vanishes. Scramble through the oak brush and cactus toward

Fremont Peak from radio tower—Fremont Peak Trail

the low point on the ridge, which will be to the right of Fremont Peak. Once you regain the ridge, follow the ridge east to the top of Fremont Peak (7,233'). Enjoy the views of Cañon City, Pikes Peak, and the Royal Gorge.

If you don't mind some additional ups and downs in elevation and a bit of rock scrambling, continue east along the ridge for another 0.5 mile for a really great view of Cañon City. You can't get lost on this trip if you stay on the road and the ridge. Use the radio tower and building, or Pikes Peak to the north, as guides if necessary.

McINTYRE HILLS

General description: An extraordinary canyon without an official trail in a proposed wilderness area.

Elevation gain: 1,500'

Elevations: Highest: 7,460' Lowest: 5,960'

Miles (one way to nearest road): 5

Rating: Easy to moderate

USGS topo map: McIntyre Hills

Users: Hikers

Road directions: From the junction of Pueblo Boulevard and US 50 in Pueblo, drive 50.5 miles west on US 50 to Five Points Campground. From Parkdale the Five Points Campground is 7.25 miles west on US 50. If you don't plan to camp, park on the north side of the highway in the day-use area. A Colorado Annual State Parks Pass is required, or a $2.00 per person hiking fee.

About 17,000 acres of the McIntyre Hills has been proposed as a Wilderness Study Area. You may see bighorn sheep at the mouth of the canyon. McIntyre Hills is also home to mountain lions, black bears, mule deer, wild turkey, and small mammals. Golden eagles and prairie falcons nest in the region.

After you've paid the necessary fees, hike through the underpass to the south side of US 50. A rocky wash comes adjacent to the paved trail. Leave the paved trail to begin your hike into **McIntyre Hills** up this wash. This canyon, which leads directly south from US 50, is primitive hiking with no official trail but provides a pleasant outing into a beautiful and rugged area. There are side canyons to explore, but for the most part you'll have no problem following the main canyon for the first 4.0 miles. You should follow a topographic map to keep track of your location. At 4.0 miles different canyons can be followed to various roads that penetrate the area from Copper Gulch Road, which heads south from Parkdale off of US 50. The nearest road is reached from a side canyon at 4.0 miles. You'll probably miss the canyon if you've not been following the map. If you're not familiar with the roads from Copper Gulch, it's best to retrace your steps back to Five Points instead of planning a pickup at the upper end, because there are many roads in the area and they are not passable when wet. Some of these roads are not great even when dry.

TRAILS FROM TEMPLE CANYON ROAD

Road directions: Temple Canyon Road gives access to **B.F. Rockafellow Ecology Park, Temple Canyon Trail** and **The Tights.** To reach Temple Canyon Road, drive to the west end of Cañon City on US 50 and turn south onto First Street, just west of Veterans Park. Cross the railroad track and the Arkansas River. Stay on First Street up the hill and past the cemetery. A mile from US 50 the road forks. Take the right fork onto Fremont County Road 3. This is Temple Canyon Road. The B.F. Rockafellow Ecology Park is 0.7 mile up Fremont County Road 3 on the right side. Continuing on Fremont County Road 3, you'll find a stone statue at the top of the hill 5.5 miles from US 50. Another 0.6 mile brings you to the east boundary of Temple Canyon Park, where Temple Canyon Trail and The Tights are located.

B.F. ROCKAFELLOW ECOLOGY PARK

General description: A trail system that has been built on top of an old landfill with access to Grape Creek.

Elevation loss (regained on return trip): 200'

Elevations: Highest: 5,600' Lowest: 5,400'

Miles (figure-eight trails only): 2.0

Rating: Easy

USGS topo maps: Cañon City, Royal Gorge (7.5')

Users: Horses, mountain bikers, hikers

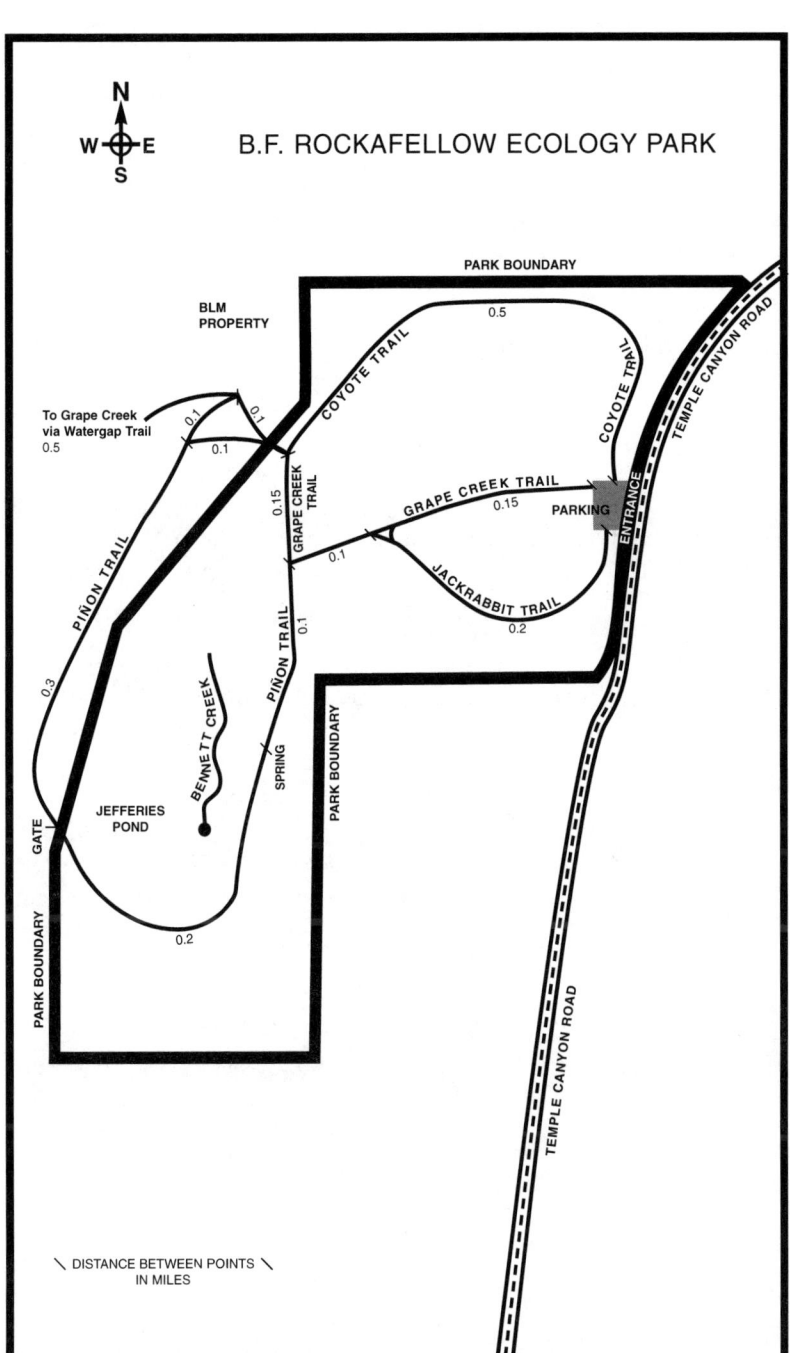

The **B.F. Rockafellow Ecology Park** trail system was conceived by the Cañon City High School Environmental Club. The park is on top of a 50-year landfill, which was closed in 1993, then covered with 18 inches of soil and reseeded. The area has been developed without taxpayer dollars. It has mostly been student labor with the help of 4-H Clubs, Boy Scouts, and Cañon City Noon Lions Club. The park is open from dawn to dusk. Several picnic tables are provided. There is a spring but don't drink the water, which has a high bacteria count. Alcoholic beverages are not allowed.

The park contains four trails plus **Watergap Trail**, which leads to Grape Creek. **Jackrabbit Trail** leaves the south end of the parking area and in 0.2 mile joins **Grape Creek Trail**, which leaves the parking area to the west. **Coyote Trail** leaves the parking area to the north and intersects **Piñon Trail** and Grape Creek Trail in 0.5 mile.

The trails in the park form a figure eight, with Jackrabbit Trail as an alternate route from the parking area instead of using the Grape Creek Trail. Watergap Trail, which is outside the park, leaves the Piñon Trail 0.1 mile beyond the intersection of Grape Creek, Coyote and Piñon Trails at the north end of the "waist" of the figure eight (refer to the map). Watergap Trail leads to Grape Creek in 0.5 mile. Once at Grape Creek you can follow a trail and road downstream 1.0 mile to the Arkansas River. You'll need to make one crossing of Grape Creek 0.2 mile before reaching the Arkansas River. Once there you can continue up the Arkansas River for 0.3 mile.

Because of the figure-eight pattern of the park trails, Watergap Trail, the trail/road along Grape Creek, and a few side roads and trails in the area, this is a fun area to explore, but please respect the private property signs.

TEMPLE CANYON TRAIL

General description: A short hike with a creek crossing and some rock scrambling needed to reach a shallow cavern known as the Temple.

Elevation gain (round trip):   700'

Elevations: Highest: 6,080'   Lowest: 5,690'

Miles (round trip to the Temple only):   1.5

Rating: Easy

USGS topo map: Royal Gorge (7.5')

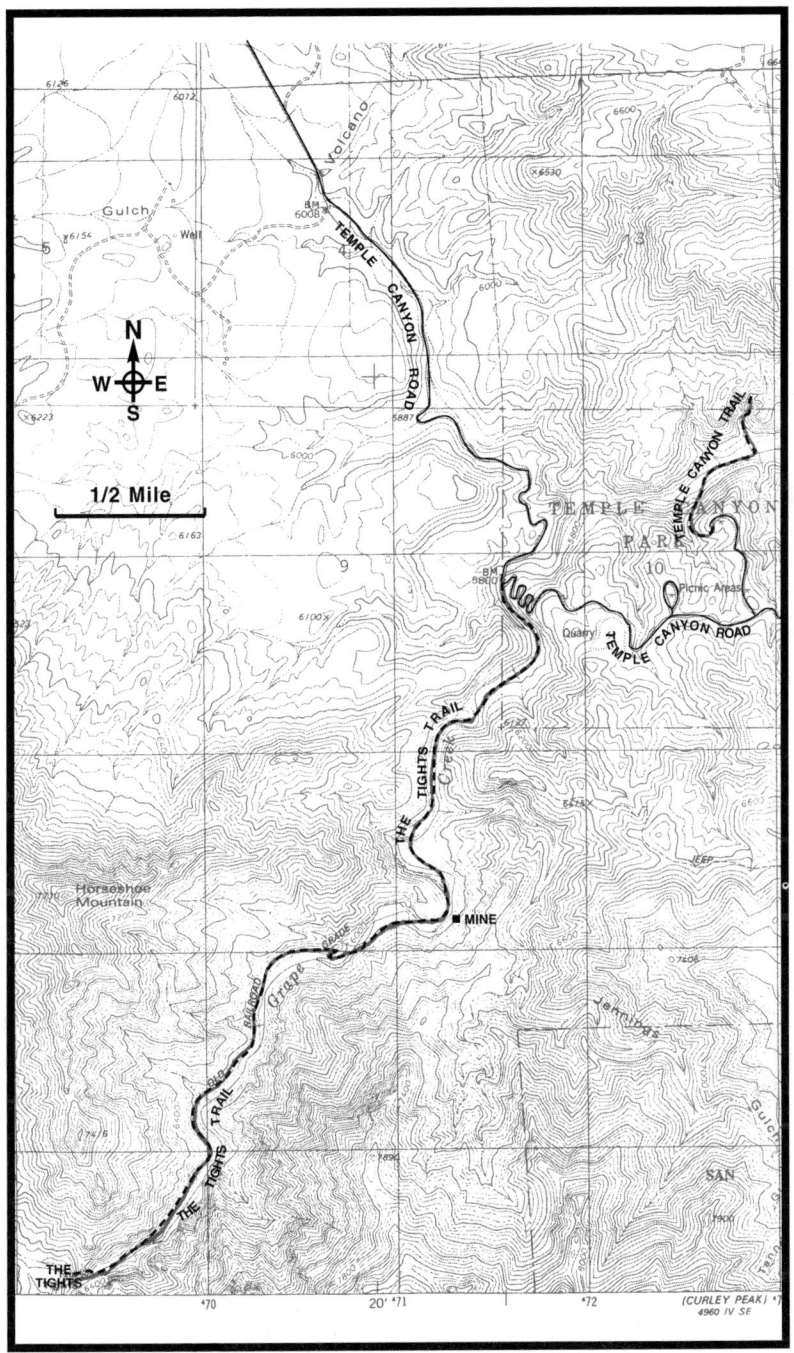

Users: Hikers

More road directions: Temple Ridge Picnic Area is 0.2 mile inside the east boundary of Temple Canyon Park. Drive to the end of the road in the picnic area (0.4 mile) to park.

A short trail up the hill to the north leads to a nice overlook of Grape Creek and the Temple Canyon area across the creek. The **Temple Canyon Trail** is to the south, just east of the table facilities, and begins just beyond two metal poles and a fence post placed alongside the trailhead area. The trail wraps around the hillside, quickly taking you north and down to Grape Creek in about 0.3 mile. Once at the creek, hike downstream about 0.1 mile to a ravine that is on the north side of the creek. Cross Grape Creek here and follow the trail up into the ravine. Watch for a second ravine on the right. A bit of rock scrambling is required to gain this northeast ravine, which leads the last few feet to the Temple. Retrace your steps to the car or continue up the ravine past the Temple (it's a scramble) and pick out an alternate route back to Grape Creek. If Grape Creek is not too high it's fun to explore along the creek. This will require many creek crossings, so wading shoes and a hiking stick are very helpful.

Grape Creek—Temple Canyon Trail

THE TIGHTS

General description: A scenic trail, mostly on an old railroad bed, that crosses Grape Creek several times to reach a narrow canyon called The Tights.

Elevation gain: 600'

Elevations: Highest: 6,400' Lowest: 5,800'

Miles (round trip): 7

Rating: Easy

USGS topo map: Royal Gorge (7.5')

Users: Motorcyclists, mountain bikers, hikers

More road directions: Temple Canyon Road crosses Grape Creek 7.7 miles from US 50 in Cañon City. The crossing is 1.6 miles west of Temple Canyon Park's east boundary at the bottom of several switchbacks. Park on the east side of the bridge. A vault toilet is available at the bridge.

The trail to **The Tights**, a narrow canyon, begins on the east side of Grape Creek, just before the bridge crossing. The trail offers some beautiful canyon vistas and a couple of nice waterfalls, for which you should take a camera. Sturdy shoes that don't mind getting wet and a walking stick will make the hike more pleasant. Because of the creek crossings the trail is not recommended during high water.

The trail is mostly an old railroad bed that over time has fallen into disrepair. The Tights Trail can be followed a short distance upstream right next to the creek, but the path soon ends, and you'll need to scramble up a steep embankment to the main road. It's best to leave the parking area on the high road, which is blocked by a pile of large rocks. The trail follows Grape Creek upstream for the first 0.5 mile, where it then crosses the creek. From here the old railroad bed continues along the west side of the creek to The Tights. Rock slides and washouts have obliterated part of the original bed, causing the current trail to take some shortcuts that add four additional creek crossings before reaching The Tights.

The trail crosses Grape Creek again at Mile 1.1 and Mile 1.2. At Mile 1.4, an old mine can be found high up on the east bank. The trail crosses the creek a fourth time at Mile 1.5. After the fifth creek crossing at Mile 1.8, the trail stays on the railroad bed on the west side of the creek for 1.5 miles to The Tights. Hiking through the

The Tights on Grape Creek—The Tights Trail

narrow canyon itself will require three more creek crossings in 0.2 mile. With so many creek crossings, this is a great place to go when the temperature is expected to be 90°F or above.

TRAILS FROM THE OAK CREEK GRADE ROAD (FREMONT COUNTY ROAD 143)

Road directions to the Oak Creek Grade Road: The Oak Creek Grade Road south of Cañon City offers four trails: **East Pierce Gulch, Lion Canyon—Highline Trail, Stultz Trail, and Tanner Trail**. The Oak Creek Grade Road can be reached by driving south on CO 115 (9th Street) from CO 50 for 1.25 miles. CO 115 at this point makes an abrupt turn to the east. Turn right (west) onto Elm Avenue and drive 0.2 mile, then turn south onto the Oak Creek Grade Road. Note that the Oak Creek Campground is 12.0 miles from here.

EAST PIERCE GULCH

General description: A seldom used trail that is a remnant of bygone days.

Option #1: *Elevation gain from Grape Creek to saddle between East and West Pierce Gulches:* 700'

    Elevations: Highest: 7,500' Lowest: 6,800'

    Miles (round trip): 4.4

Option #2: *Elevation gain from Grape Creek to 1 mile down West Pierce Gulch:* 1,040'

    Elevations: Highest: 7,500' Lowest: 6,800'

    Miles (round trip): 6.4

Rating: Easy

USGS topo maps: Curley Peak, Iron Mountain

Users: Horses, hikers

More road directions: Technically, this trail is beyond the 50.0-mile drive from Pueblo but is included for your information. Grape Creek Access Road #6227 is at Yorkville (site) 2.0 miles beyond the entrance to the Oak Creek Campground. This access road is 49.0 miles from the junction of Pueblo Boulevard and US 50 in Pueblo.

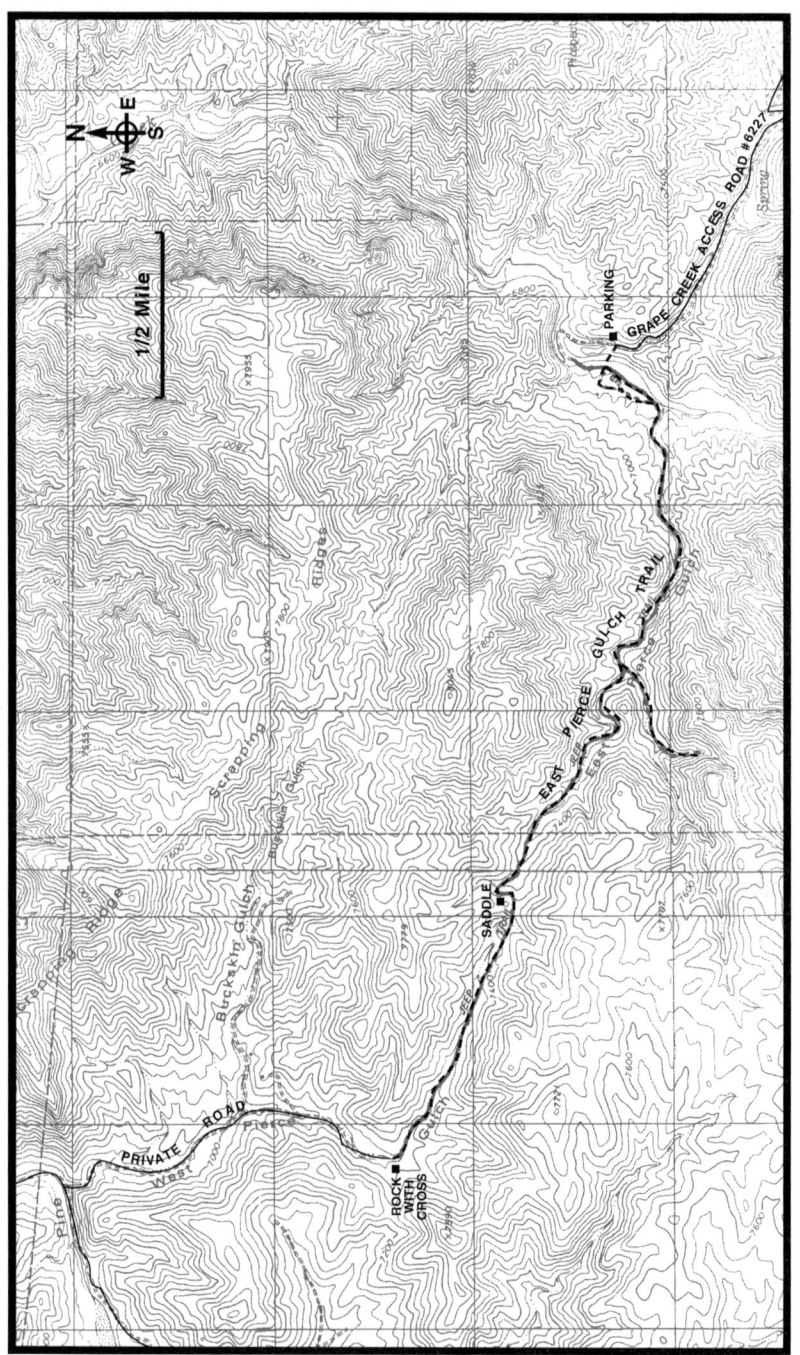

It's another 3.9 miles to the trailhead on a road that requires cautious driving. The first 1.1 miles is private property—**please stay on the road**. Parts of the road can be muddy and rough, so use your best judgment when driving. There are a few parking areas along the way that can be used as a starting point for your hike.

Assuming you've made it to the end of Road #6227 above Grape Creek, your first challenge in hiking **East Pierce Gulch** will be to wade across Grape Creek. This trail is not recommended during spring runoff or any time that the creek may be running high. The trail is an old jeep road that at one time crossed Grape Creek but is now washed out, so crossing must be done on foot. When the creek is high it is a dangerous crossing. This is a Wilderness Study Area, so motorized vehicles are not allowed.

Remnants of stone structure along Grape Creek—East Pierce Gulch Trail

Before beginning your hike, read the information sign in the parking area. In May of 1999 there was a "Killer from the Hills." This flash flood totally washed out the last 0.2 mile of road to Grape Creek. By hiking down the steep embankment to the right of the sign, you can still hike the wash north to Grape Creek. The new trail leaves the parking area to the northwest. Before descending the short but somewhat steep trail to Grape Creek, look west across the creek to the two old stone structures along the creek. To the right of the two structures is a faint road leading up the hill towards a meadow, which is separated from the stone structures by a narrow band of trees. At the right edge of the meadow are the remnants of an old cabin. You may wish to explore this area on your return trip.

Once across the creek, take time to examine what remains of the two old stone structures. These structures are possibly remnants of Iron Mountain mining days. Continue your hike upstream for 0.2 mile and note that just before dropping down the small hill into the East Pierce Gulch wash, you'll see another road heading uphill to the right (north-northeast) away from the wash. This road leads to the cabin in the meadow and continues to the stone structures at Grape Creek.

At the bottom of the East Pierce Gulch wash, the road forks. The left fork goes down the wash toward Grape Creek, while the other fork crosses the wash to climb up the hill on the opposite side. These roads can be explored on the return trip. Leave the road at this point (turn right), and begin your hike up the wash.

At 0.5 mile up the East Pierce Gulch wash a side gully comes in from the left. At 0.8 mile up the wash is the first remnant of the old road that has long since disappeared from the lower portion of the gulch. At 0.9 mile a second gully comes in from the left at a sharp bend in East Pierce Gulch. This grass-covered gully, which is straight ahead as you hike up East Pierce Gulch, beckons. It's worth exploring, but go right to continue up East Pierce Gulch. The road may not be apparent at this point, but once picked up again, it continues along the wash, sometimes in the wash, at times crossing the wash, until just below the saddle, where it pulls out of the gulch to reach the saddle at 7,500'. It is a total of 2.0 miles up East Pierce Gulch to the saddle.

From the saddle you can hike 1.0 mile down West Pierce Gulch before the road turns north and enters private property. A rock painted with a white cross is the turnaround point. This first mile is fairly primitive and a nice hike, but you'll need to regain 340' in elevation. If you continue beyond the first mile, the road becomes fairly well maintained, giving access to private homes. There are no signs to tell you that you've left Bureau of Land Management lands, but a locked gate at Pine Gulch 2.25 miles below the saddle will let you know that you are trespassing. Get permission to hike the lower 1.25 miles. You may wish to turn around at the saddle to allow time for exploring the side gullies or roads you passed along the way.

Cows may be seen grazing along Grape Creek and in East Pierce

Gulch. Pockets of soft sand in the wash and on the road make this a miserable mountain bike trip.

LION CANYON—HIGHLINE TRAIL #1329

General description: A pleasant forest hike with great views of the Sangre de Cristo Mountains from the top.

Elevation gain: 1,520'

Elevations: Highest: 9,160' Lowest: 7,640'

Miles (Oak Creek Campground to Locke Park—one way): 3

Rating: Moderate

USGS topo map: Curley Peak

Users: Motorcyclists, mountain bikers, horses, hikers

More road directions: The Lion Canyon—Highline Trail is reached from the Oak Creek Campground. Drive to the trailhead parking area on the loop at the end of the campground road.

The **Lion Canyon Trail** follows a small, intermittent creek for 3.0 miles to Locke Park. The trail crosses the creek several times but should present no problems. This trail, technically called the Highline Trail, becomes a 4-wheel-drive road in Locke Park which can be followed for 10.0 miles via Forest Road 274, Forest Road 336 past Adobe Peak, and Forest Road 315 to its other end, which is known as the Lewis Creek Trail (see "Wetmore Area" section).

Pack a lunch for your hike to Locke Park. When you get there, relax under a nice big shady pine tree at the edge of the meadow and marvel at the beauty of the Sangre de Cristo Mountains. If cows are in the area, please leave them alone.

STULTZ TRAIL #1334

General description: A trail through scrub oak, forest, and meadow, which mostly follows a ridge and which intersects the Tanner Trail at its end; climbing Curley Peak is a nice option.

Elevation gain, Stultz Trail only: 2,525'

Elevations: Highest: 9,440' Lowest: 6,915'

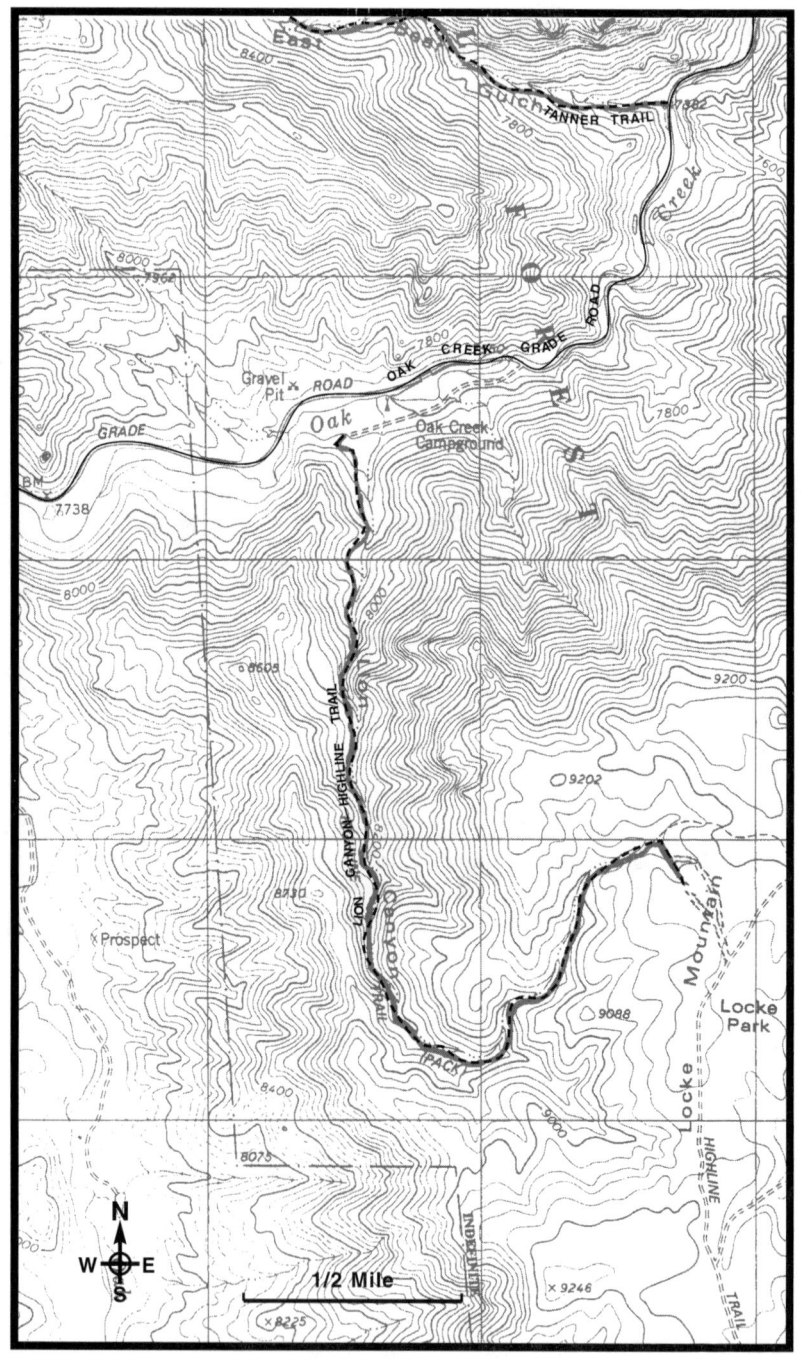

Miles (round trip): 10

Rating: Moderately difficult

USGS topo maps: Curley Peak, Rockvale

Users: All-terrain vehicles, motorcyclists, horses, hikers

More road directions: The Stultz Trail #1334 begins at approximately the 8-mile marker on the Oak Creek Grade Road. When you're at the 8-mile marker you're 0.1 mile beyond the parking area for the Stultz Trail. There is a sign marking the trailhead. The parking area is marked Forest Road 348 and is across the Oak Creek Grade Road from the Stultz Trail.

Stultz Trail tends to be filled with loose rock, so wear sturdy hiking boots. The trail has shortcuts used by motorcyclists and sections that have been rerouted. The shortcuts and some old trail sections can be used but they tend to be steep and torn up. Most of these side trails are blocked by dirt mounds, rocks, or logs to discourage their use. The main trail has been graded four feet wide, is more gradual, and is definitely preferred for hiking. It is wise to keep an eye on the weather since much of the trail is along ridges, in open areas of scrub oak, or in meadows, so lightning could pose a real threat. The loose rock will slow your pace if you're trying to outrun a storm.

At Mile 4.5, in an open park to the right of the trail, are the remnants of an old cabin. A few yards farther are the remains of yet another structure. At Mile 4.75, a trail branches off to the left. This is a shortcut to the base of Curley Peak. Take the right fork to stay on the Stultz Trail. At Mile 5.0, the Stultz Trail ends at Tanner Trail #1333. This offers a wide variety of choices involving the Tanner Trail, including climbing Curley Peak (9,622'), hiking through Chute Park to Tanner Peak, and/or making loop trips with cars spotted at each end of your chosen route (see "Tanner Trail" section).

Some maps show a trail beginning at Stultz Gulch and joining the Stultz Trail at Mile 2.5. The Oak Creek Grade end of this trail is private property with no trail access. You may see the remnants of this trail as it leaves the Stultz Trail. Stay on the Stultz Trail.

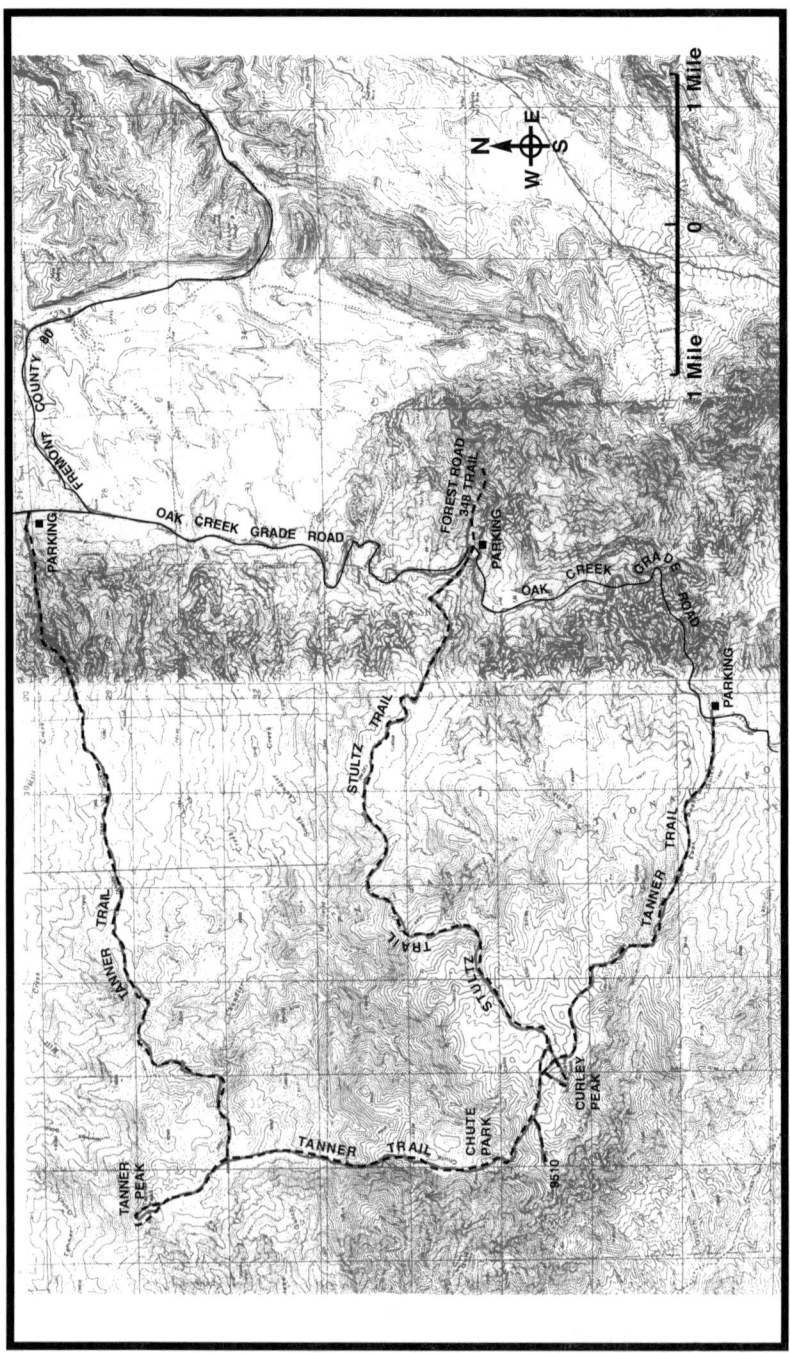

STULTZ TRAIL—FOREST ROAD 348

General description: A short, overgrown trail on a ridge to the east of the parking area that offers good experience in trail finding.

Elevation gain: 217'

Elevations: Highest: 6,917' Lowest: 6,700'

Miles (round trip): 1

Rating: Easy

USGS topo map: Rockvale

Starting from the **Stultz Trail** parking area, two very short trails can be explored. The trail (road) leaving the south end of the parking lot has been blocked to cars by a wood fence that has walk-through access to the left of the trail. This trail wraps around the hill and stops in a gully just below the parking area.

The road east from the parking area, in 0.1 mile, forms a circular turnaround and campfire site. A side road to the south of this turnaround heads up the hill to another campfire spot. The road off the east end of the turnaround is the beginning of a trail that runs downhill and east for about 0.5 mile along a ridge. This trail has become very overgrown with scrub oak and cactus plants, but can be followed with moderate difficulty for about half its length. The trail disappears after that but the ridge is clearly visible. It's a good experience in trail finding. Pay attention because it's just as hard to find the trail on the way back. If you stay on top of the ridge you'll be okay, but a few looks backward on the way out will identify landmarks for the return trip.

TANNER TRAIL #1333

General description: A rugged trail with one trailhead at North Cow Creek and one at East Bear Gulch, with some spectacular views, and with the option of climbing Curley or Tanner Peaks, or, if two cars are available, hiking a loop trip using Stultz Trail.

Users: All-terrain vehicles, motorcyclists, hikers

Favorite Option #1:
Elevation gain from North Cow Creek trailhead to Tanner Peak (round trip): 4,280'

Elevations: Highest: 9,340'   Lowest: 5,960'

Miles (round trip): 13.5

Rating: Difficult

USGS topo maps: Curley Peak, Rockvale

Favorite Option #2:

Elevation gain from East Bear Gulch trailhead to Curley Peak: 2,260'

Elevations: Highest: 9,622'   Lowest: 7,362'

Miles (round trip): 7

Rating: Moderate

USGS topo map: Curley Peak

Favorite Option #3:

Elevation gain from East Bear Gulch trailhead to Stultz trailhead (loop): 2,080'

Elevation gain from Stultz trailhead to East Bear Gulch trailhead (loop): 2,525'

Elevations: Highest: 9,440'
Lowest (Stultz trailhead): 6,915'
East Bear Gulch trailhead: 7,362'

Miles (for loop): 8.5

Rating: Moderate

USGS topo maps: Curley Peak, Rockvale

Option #4:

Elevation gain from East Bear Gulch trailhead to Tanner Peak (round trip): 3,600'

Elevations: Highest: 9,480' (near Curley Peak)
Lowest: 7,362'

Miles (round trip): 14

Rating: Difficult

USGS topo map: Curley Peak

Option #5:

Elevation gain from East Bear Gulch trailhead with side trip to Tanner Peak, then to North Cow Creek trailhead: 3,090'

Elevations: Highest: 9,480' (near Curley Peak)
Lowest (North Cow Creek trailhead): 5,960'

Miles (for loop): 13.75

Rating: Difficult

USGS topo maps: Curley Peak, Rockvale

More road directions: Tanner Trail #1333 forms a 12.25-mile semi-circular loop with one leg on the Oak Creek Grade Road at 3.9 miles and the other leg 7.1 miles farther at mile marker 11. The northern end of the loop begins at North Cow Creek. A trailhead sign and an off-road parking area are provided. Please note that the former trailhead at Mill Creek is closed to the public. The Tanner trailhead at East Bear Gulch (mile marker 11) has good parking in the meadow across the road.

The **Tanner Trail** can be steep and rocky, so wear good footwear. The weather can be hot and dry, or it can be wet and cold, with violent thunder and lightning storms. So be prepared with plenty of water and appropriate clothing.

A favorite trip is to climb Tanner Peak on the northern section of the trail from North Cow Creek. Likewise, climbing Curley Peak on the Tanner Trail up East Bear Gulch is popular. And because the Tanner Trail has two trailheads, with the Stultz Trail intersecting it near the East Bear Gulch end, loop hikes can be made if cars are placed at the appropriate trailheads. A pleasant trip is to place a car at the Stultz trailhead and drive another vehicle to the Tanner trailhead at East Bear Gulch. You can hike up East Bear Gulch, climb Curley Peak, then return to your vehicle via the Stultz Trail. Or you can reverse this loop trip.

The northern section of the trail, beginning at North Cow Creek, passes through private property for the first 0.5 mile. Stay on the trail. At Mile 1.5 there is a fenced, but very deep, open mining pit. Watch dogs and small children. At Mile 5.0, the trail loses about 300' elevation as it drops 0.3 mile down to Chandler Creek, which flows intermittently. It's a 0.6-mile and 600'-climb out of Chandler Creek to the trail junction that will take you north (right) via a side trail to Tanner Peak or south (left) through Chute Park.

Tanner Peak from junction of Tanner Trail and side trail to the peak

Tanner Peak (9,340'), 0.75 mile away, is visible to the north from this junction. If you're climbing Tanner Peak, the side trail splits at the base of the peak, with the trail to the left (west) heading straight up the mountain. The trail to the right skirts the mountain to the east and reaches the peak from the north. This trail is longer but is not so steep and you'll pass the remnants of two old cabins. At the north end of the peak, when the trail begins to turn south for the final ascent, leave the trail heading north to break free of the trees for a great view of Fremont Peak, US 50, Skyline Drive, Cañon City, and Pikes Peak. From the top of Tanner Peak, the magnificent Sangre de Cristo Mountains rise to the west, while Chute Park and Curley Peak lie to the south. Return to the beginning of the loop by hiking down the south face of the peak and then retrace your steps to the Tanner Trail.

Back at the junction of the side trail to Tanner Peak and the continuation of Tanner Trail through Chute Park, one can hike 2.75 miles through Chute Park to the Tanner Trail and Stultz Trail junction (see "Stultz Trail" section). If you opt to hike through Chute Park, you'll lose at least 315' elevation, then gain at least 810' before reaching the Tanner and Stultz Trails junction. This is one of the prettiest sections of the Tanner Trail, with great views of the Sangre de Cristo Mountains and the Grape Creek drainage area.

The lowest point on this section of trail is 0.7 mile from the trail junction to Tanner Peak. The northern edge of Chute Park is another 0.7 mile. The trail through Chute Park is an easy 0.4 mile, but the park can be hot when the temperature soars or become deadly in a thunder and lightning storm. Chute Park is an incredibly beautiful flower garden. The trail continues south for another 0.2 mile to the bottom of a very steep and rocky 0.5-mile section. Slightly more than half of the elevation gain on this section of the trail is here. At the top of the steep section, a side trail (right fork) goes out to a 9,510' point in 0.3 mile. The view is worth the side trip. From the junction of the Tanner Trail and this side trail, it is another 0.25 mile east to the Tanner and Stultz Trails junction.

Curley Peak (9,622'), which lies to the south of the Tanner/Stultz Trails junction, does not have a trail to the top but can be climbed from several places near the junction.

Continuing south 0.2 mile on the Tanner Trail from the Tanner/Stultz Trails junction, the trail intersects a well-worn path. This path is a shortcut from the Stultz Trail (0.15 mile to the east) to the base of Curley Peak. You cannot reach the top of Curley Peak from this path, but there is a nice campsite (without water) located at a rocky outcrop of Curley Peak.

Tanner Peak and Chute Park from 9,510' point—Tanner Trail

From the junction with this path the Tanner Trail heads south and east, staying fairly level for 0.8 mile before beginning the steep descent down East Bear Gulch where, after 2.5 miles and a 1,840' elevation drop, you reach the Oak Creek Grade Road at mile marker 11.

Looking west to Curley Peak—Tanner Trail

TRAILS FROM FREMONT COUNTY ROAD 9

Road directions: Fremont County Road 9 is best reached by driving north 0.7 mile on North Raynolds Avenue from US 50 in east Cañon City, then 0.1 mile west (left) on Pear Street to Field Avenue. Turn right onto Field Avenue and drive north 2.4 miles, where it becomes Fremont County Road 9. This road is a Gold Belt Tour—Scenic Byway. Dinosaurs once roamed this land. At Mile 3.2 from the junction of Fremont County Road 9 and Field Avenue is the Cleveland Quarry Recreation Site. This is a day-use area with dinosaur exhibits, tables, and restrooms. A quarter mile beyond, reached by either hiking trail or Fremont County Road 9, is a second exhibit area with parking. From here a 0.25-mile trail takes you to the Marsh Quarry. Several signs along the trail add insight to this interesting area. Take time to hike the short trail and to read the informational signs at both areas before driving the last 3.6 miles to the **Red Canyon Park** entrance or the 6.4 miles to the **Sand Gulch** area trails.

RED CANYON PARK

USGS topo maps: Cooper Mountain, Rice Mountain

There are no established trails in the park, but you can make your own trails as others have done by exploring the gullies and ridges. The park has some interesting red rock formations with some spires reaching 100 feet. There are two picnic areas with restrooms.

Red Canyon Park

SAND GULCH AREA

General description: Features a technical climber's paradise and a delightful place to hike, picnic, and camp. Vegetation includes cholla and prickly pear cacti, and juniper trees.

Rating: Easy

Users: Climbers, hikers

Overview and more road directions: The entrance to the Sand Gulch area is on the west (left) side of Fremont County Road 9. After crossing the cattle guard, follow the signs 0.3 mile to the Sand Gulch

Campground and park in the day-use parking lot, where Bureau of Land Management signs give an overview of this technical climbing area. Signs mark trailheads and trail junctions. There are three trailheads in the campground—**Sand Gulch, The Gallery,** and **Free Form Wall**. While hiking at the climbing walls, be especially considerate of the climbers and keep your pets on a leash.

SAND GULCH TRAILS

Elevation gain from Sand Gulch Campground to Road #5825:   600'

Elevations: Highest: 7,000'   Lowest: 6,400'

Miles (one way):   2

USGS topo maps: Cooper Mountain, Cripple Creek South, High Park

    A number of options are available from the **Sand Gulch Trail** because it links with the Contest Wall Trail, the Free Form Wall Trail, and Road #5825. The Sand Gulch Trail leaves the campground from the day-use parking area and drops immediately into Sand Gulch (topographic maps name this Espinosa Gulch). At the bottom of the gulch turn right (north). The Sand Gulch Trail follows the bottom of the gully.

    The **Contest Wall Trail** junction, marked by a sign, is about 0.2 mile up the gully. The Contest Wall Trail is good, but rugged, with steps and switchbacks as it climbs steeply to the base of the climbing wall. It then follows the base of the wall for perhaps 0.3 mile before descending to the bottom of the gulch and its junction with the Sand Gulch Trail and Free Form Wall Trail.

    If you're not hiking the Contest Wall Trail and opt to stay in the gully on the Sand Gulch Trail, some rock scrambling is necessary, but not difficult. After about another 0.4 mile up the gully, a sign marks the junction of the Free Form Wall Trail to the right and the Contest Wall Trail to the left.

    The **Free Form Wall Trail** at this junction switchbacks to the base of the wall. Once at the base of the wall the trail can be explored north (left) for a short distance before it ends. To return to the campground turn right (south). Continue to follow the trail along the wall. There's a nice view of the campground and valley just before the trail cuts around the end of the wall and begins its descent to the group campsite.

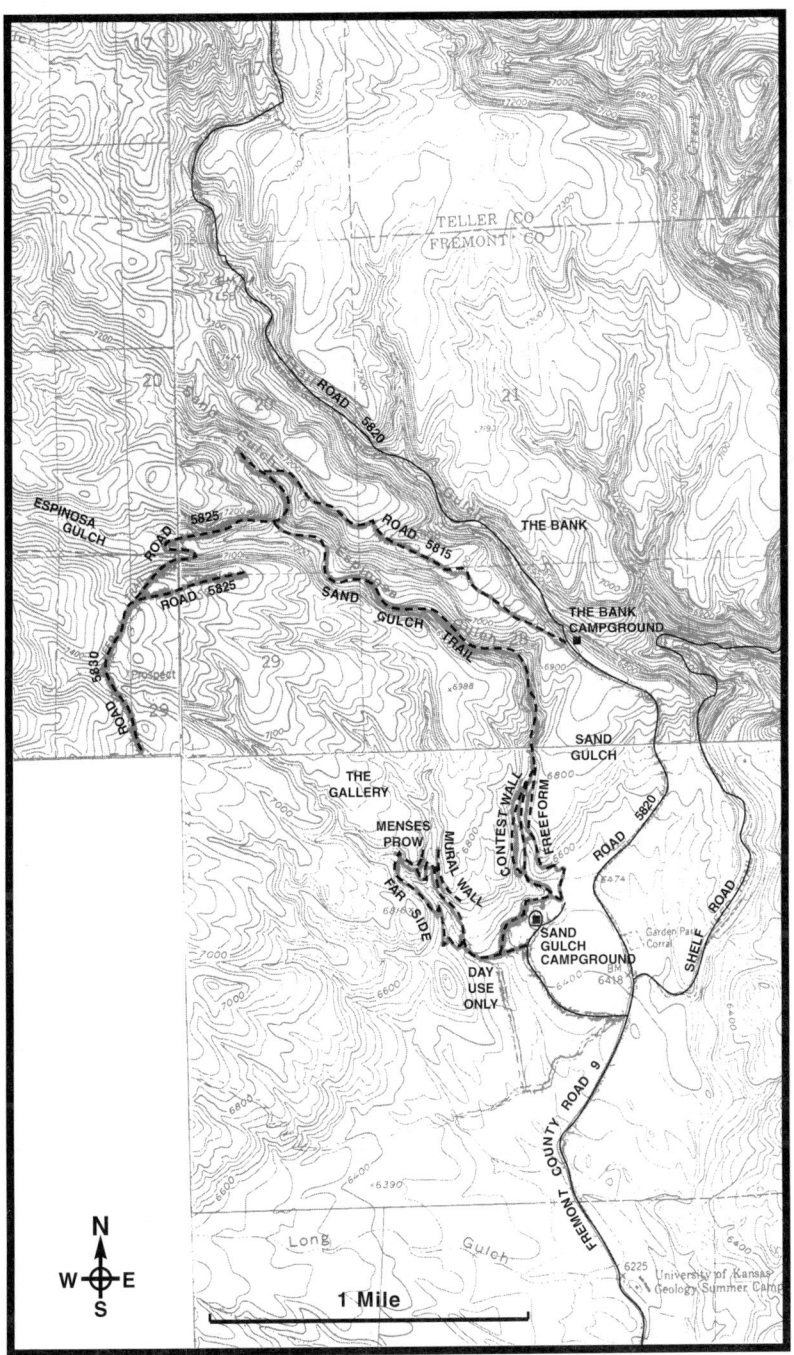

Contest Wall—Sand Gulch Trail

From the junction of the Sand Gulch Trail with the Contest Wall and Free Form Wall Trails, continue on the Sand Gulch Trail another 1.5 miles in the gully to Road #5825. Road #5825 can be followed to the left (west) 0.4 mile up Espinosa Gulch, where it switchbacks, climbs to the ridge top, and comes to the junction of Roads #5825 and #5830 in 0.3 mile. Road #5825 dead-ends in 0.5 mile in the meadows above Espinosa and Sand Gulches. Road #5830 is more appropriately explored on wheels.

If Road #5825 is hiked to the right from Sand Gulch Trail, it ends at Road #5815 in 0.2 mile. Road #5815 continues northwest (left) for 0.1 mile, where it dead-ends at the Sand Gulch wash. The hike can be continued up the wash.

Road #5815 can be hiked southeast (right) along the ridge between Sand Gulch and Trail Gulch for 1.25 miles to Road #5820 at The Bank Campground. From The Bank Campground it is another 1.9 miles via the road back to your car at Sand Gulch Campground (see "The Bank" description below).

THE GALLERY TRAILS

Elevation gain for Gallery loop: 280'

Elevations: Highest: 6,680'   Lowest: 6,400'

Miles (loop trip): 1.5

USGS topo map: Cooper Mountain

Far Side, Menses Prow, and Mural climbing walls are found in **The Gallery.** A nice 1.5-mile loop trip can be hiked using these climbing wall trails. The Gallery trailhead is between campsites #9 and #10 as one enters the campground. The trail drops down to Sand Gulch, then crosses it. In a few feet the trail crosses the small creek that drains the Gallery area, and then passes through a day-use area which can be reached by a primitive road (the left fork after the cattle guard crossing at Fremont County Road 9). The trail crosses the Gallery drainage again and follows a fence line for a few feet. The first junction reached is the bottom of the loop. The trail to the left drops to the creek drainage, then climbs to the Far Side climbing wall. The trail to the right leads to Mural Wall and Menses Prow.

The Mural Wall and Menses Prow Trail forks in 0.25 mile. The right fork leads to the Mural Wall and can be explored as a side trip. The left fork, after crossing a creek drainage, continues to the base of Menses Prow. At the base of Menses Prow go left to continue the loop trip. Once on the west side of Menses Prow, watch for a trail leading down to a creek drainage. Take the trail to the drainage, where a short side trail crosses the drainage and leads to some magnificent boulders. The loop trail from this junction continues a short distance down the creek bed before ascending to the base of the Far Side climbing wall. A hike along the Far Side wall and a few switchbacks complete the loop. The trail offers some nice views of the valley below.

THE BANK

More road directions: More climbing walls and trails are located at The Bank. To reach The Bank from Sand Gulch Campground, return to Fremont County Road 9. Drive north 0.1 mile and take Road #5820, passing the corral. The Bank Campground is 1.0 mile beyond the corral. Stay on Road #5820 to the day-use parking area. Just beyond the parking area, the road forks. The fork downhill to the right is Road #5820 and leads to the **Dark Wall Trail** (0.1 mile) and the **Surreal Estate Wall Trail** (0.3 mile). The fork to the left is Road #5815 from Sand Gulch (see "Sand Gulch Trail" description). Hiking these roads is an option, but they might be better negotiated on a mountain bike, on an all-terrain vehicle, or in a high-clearance 4-wheel-drive vehicle.

COLORADO SPRINGS AREA

Colorado Springs has trails within the city limits and the surrounding area. These trails have been adequately described in *Trails Guide: Denver to Pikes Peak*, by Zoltan Malocsay; the "El Paso County Regional Parks and Trails" brochure; and the Colorado Lottery Web site at www.coloradolottery.com/about/trailmaps. A selected few of these trails are described here for your convenience and to open the door to other possibilities in this region.

The Garden of the Gods area and the Barr Trail to the top of Pikes Peak are fairly well known and are not discussed here for that reason. The Clear Spring Ranch Trail and the Fountain Creek Regional Park are included because of their proximity to Pueblo. Bear Canyon and North Cheyenne Canyon areas offer many delightful trails. These trails are well used so if you insist on hiking alone, this area is recommended, as there is bound to be someone along the trail shortly, if you encounter any problems.

CLEAR SPRING RANCH TRAIL

General description: A riparian area east of I-25, excellent for wildlife viewing.

Miles: 4.0 (north end—round trip); 2.0 (south end—loop)

Rating: Easy

Map: An information sheet with map is available at the Fountain Creek Regional Park Nature Center.

Users: Mountain bikers, hikers

Overview and road directions: The **Clear Spring Ranch Trail** is made available to the public through the collaboration of the Colorado Springs Utilities and the El Paso County Parks. The Clear Spring Ranch Trail is accessed off I-25 at Exit 123. Access to the area is limited by the number of parking spaces available. There is limited parking just east of the railroad track or at the trailhead (10 spaces). The road to the trailhead parking area may be very muddy when wet. Restroom facilities and a covered pavilion are available here. Wildlife includes rabbits, raccoons, muskrats, foxes, squirrels, coyotes, mule and white-tail deer, and over 200 species of birds. Dogs must be on a leash. Camping and fires are prohibited.

A 1.0-mile interpretive trail runs through a riparian area along Fountain Creek. From the pavilion follow the trail 0.25 mile east to the Fountain River. Once at the river, the interpretive trail runs south for about 0.5 mile to a road junction. If you are doing the loop, turn left (south) at the junction and continue south for another 0.25 mile to another junction. At this junction turn right (west) and continue to the railroad tracks where you will turn north. Follow this road north for 0.6 mile to the access road to the trailhead. From here it's 0.25 mile back to your car if you are parked at the trailhead.

If you are at the river from the trailhead and decide to go north, it is 0.3 mile on the interpretive trail before you must return to a road. Once on the road you can continue north for 1.8 miles to a utility building, which is the current end of the Clear Spring Ranch Trail. However, you can make a 1.4-mile loop beyond the utility building. Please stay on the road if you do this loop. There are some additional roads in this area that will become part of the trail system in the future and eventually this area will be connected to the Fountain Creek Regional Trail.

This riparian area is excellent for wildlife viewing, especially birding, and offers a bit of peace within sight of a busy interstate.

FOUNTAIN CREEK REGIONAL PARK

General description: A developed park for picnicking, fishing, wildlife viewing, horseback riding, biking, hiking.

Miles in park: 5.4 (some with use restrictions)

Rating: Easy

Map: Obtain map at Nature Center

Users: Horses, bicyclists, hikers (motorized vehicles prohibited)

Road directions: Please note that as of this writing, the Willow Springs Fishing Ponds area has been closed to public use due to high levels of perchloroethylene (PCE), a chemical which may be harmful to humans. The Fountain Creek Regional Trail through the area remains open. The future of this area is uncertain.

Fountain Creek Regional Park is located along Fountain Creek east of I-25. Take Exit 132 (Widefield/Security—CO 16), then go east on CO 16 for 0.5 mile and take the exit to Highway 85. Turn right (south) onto Highway 85. To reach the Willow Springs Fishing Ponds, immediately turn right again onto Willow Springs Road and drive 0.3 mile to the park entrance. There is trailhead parking south of the ponds for those who wish to ride horses or bicycles on the regional trail.

A great place to become familiar with the entire area is at the Fountain Creek Regional Park Nature Center. To reach the Nature Center continue south on Highway 85 for 0.6 mile from Willow Springs Road to Cattail Marsh Road. Turn right (west) onto Cattail Marsh Road, which becomes Pepper Grass Lane, into the Nature Center. The Nature Center is 0.2 mile from Highway 85. The Nature Center is open 9 a.m. to 4 p.m. Tuesday through Saturday and offers exhibits, programs, and slide shows about the wetland communities. A large viewing window overlooks the Cattail Marsh Wildlife Area and the mountains beyond.

Other access points to the regional trail off Highway 85, heading south from the Nature Center, are at Duckwood Road (park maintenance facility) and Lyckman Drive (Hanson Nature Park). There is access on the north end of the park at Carson Boulevard.

There is a 0.75-mile **self-guided trail**, open to pedestrians only, that circles the Willow Springs Fishing Ponds. The ponds, developed in 1989, provide fishing for trout, catfish, and bluegills. A State of Colorado fishing license is required. The nicely developed area has picnic tables, a pavilion, interpretive displays, handicap-accessible fishing docks, a playground, a fish-cleaning station, and restrooms. This is a delightful place because of the many **NO-NO'S**. The restrictions are: no firearms, no ice skating, no boating, no swimming, no alcohol, no glass containers, no golfing, no snowmobiling, and no camping. Pets must be on a leash and feces must be picked up by the owner.

The parking area south of the ponds gives access to the **Fountain Creek Regional Trail** which is open to horses, bicyclists, and hikers. From this parking area, the regional trail goes south 3.0 miles and north 4.7 miles to Academy Boulevard, where the trail continues as the Pikes Peak Greenway Trail through Colorado Springs. Pets must be on a leash at all times and feces must be picked up or scattered off the trail.

At the Nature Center, a 0.6-mile **nature trail** loop through the Cattail Marsh Wildlife Area has interpretive signs and observation overlooks. The stream, pond, marsh, and cottonwood communities offer a diverse amount of wildlife including muskrats, white-tailed deer, and many birds. Allowing plenty of time and using binoculars

A pond along the nature trail—Fountain Creek Regional Park

greatly enhances the enjoyment of this trail. The nature trail, open only to pedestrians, is accessible to wheelchairs. No dogs, bicycles, or horses are allowed.

A short side trail links the nature trail loop to the **Fountain Creek Regional Trail**. From the Nature Center the regional trail goes south for 2.4 miles, passing through the Cottonwood and Wild Plum Meadows. North from the Nature Center the trail goes 0.6 mile to the regional trail access parking at Willow Springs Fishing Ponds. Along this section of trail are two wildlife observation pavilions overlooking a pond and surrounding wetlands. Both have interpretive displays.

BEAR CREEK REGIONAL PARK

General description: A developed park for horses, bikers, and hikers with playground, picnic pavilions, nature trails, and wildlife viewing.

Miles in park: 10 (some with use restrictions)

Rating: Easy

Map: Obtain map at Nature Center

Users: Horses, bicyclists, hikers (motorized vehicles prohibited)

Road directions: To reach the Bear Creek Regional Park, take Exit 141 from I-25 and go west on US 24 (Cimarron Street) for 1.5 miles to 21st Street. Turn south onto 21st Street, driving 1.1 miles to the parking area at West Rio Grande Avenue. The park on the east side of 21st Street has many amenities, including picnic pavilions, playground, restrooms, and administrative offices. The trail west of 21st Street gives access to the Bear Creek Nature Center and Section 16 Trail. These areas can also be reached by vehicle.

The Bear Creek Nature Center may be the best place to begin your exploration of this area. The Nature Center is located at 245 Bear Creek Road, off 26th Street and Lower Gold Camp Road. If you've driven to the West Rio Grande Avenue parking area at 21st Street, turn north onto 21st Street for 0.2 mile to Lower Gold Camp Road. Drive west on Lower Gold Camp Road 1.1 miles to its intersection with 26th Street and Bear Creek Road. Turn south onto Bear Creek Road and drive 0.2 mile to the entrance to the Nature Center.

Section 16 Trail can be reached from the Nature Center on the trail system or by vehicle. By vehicle, return to the intersection of 26th Street, Bear Creek Road, and Lower Gold Camp Road. Drive west on Gold Camp Road 0.9 mile to the trailhead. The trailhead can also be reached by continuing on Bear Creek Road south of the Nature Center 0.9 mile to its junction with High Drive (one way) and Gold Camp Road. Turn right (north) onto Gold Camp Road and drive 0.2 mile to the trailhead.

The Bear Creek Nature Center offers 2.0 miles of **self-guided nature trails** open to foot traffic only (no bicycles, horses, or dogs allowed). The Songbird Trail is handicap accessible. The Bear Creek Regional Park offers a variety of nature experiences. Vegetation includes short grass prairie, scrub oak woodlands, and cottonwood riparian communities, while wildlife includes birds, black bears, deer, and coyote.

TRAILS FROM THE GOLD CAMP ROAD/HIGH DRIVE AREA

Road directions: **Bear Creek Trail, Saint Mary's Falls Trail,** and **Seven Bridges (North Cheyenne) Trail** are popular trails off the Gold Camp Road. To reach these trailheads from I-25, take Exit 138 for Circle Drive, the Broadmoor Hotel, Cheyenne Mountain Zoo, and

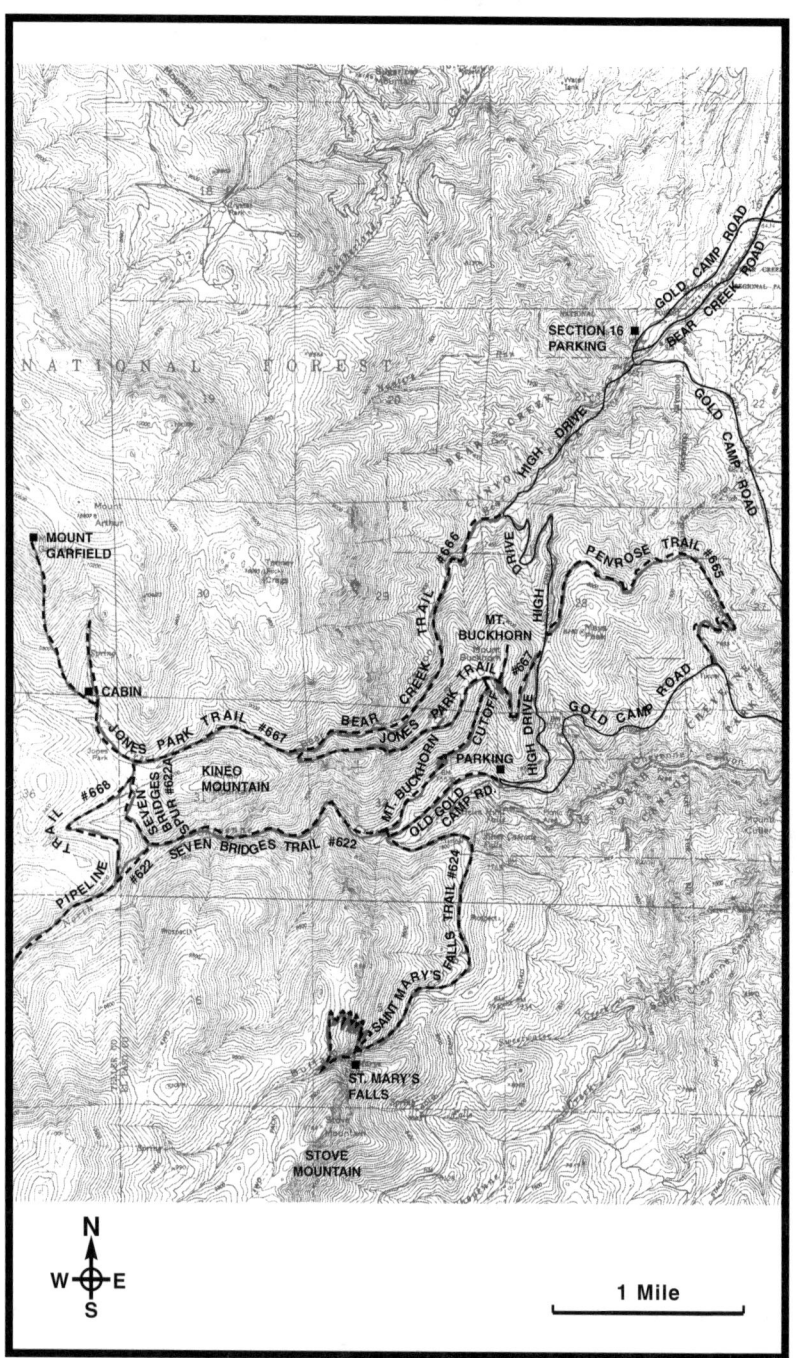

Seven Falls. Circle Drive goes to the east and Lake Avenue goes to the west. Go west on Lake Avenue for 3.0 miles to the Broadmoor. Turn right onto Lake Circle and drive 0.25 mile around the north side of the Broadmoor to Mesa. Turn right onto Mesa for 0.1 mile, then left onto Cresta. Drive 0.4 mile north on Cresta to Cheyenne Boulevard (not Cheyenne Road). Turn left (west) onto Cheyenne Boulevard and drive 1.0 mile to the Seven Falls entrance. At the Seven Falls entrance take the road to the right. This road is the entrance to North Cheyenne Canyon Park. From here it is 2.7 miles to Helen Hunt Falls and another 0.6 mile to a large, but usually crowded, parking area. High Drive, which is one way, begins from this parking area.

This parking area can also be reached using Exit 141 from I-25, driving west on US 24 (Cimarron Road) 1.5 miles to 21st Street. Turn south onto 21st Street and drive 0.9 mile to the Lower Gold Camp Road. Drive west on the Lower Gold Camp Road for 1.1 miles to its intersection with 26th Street, Bear Creek Road, and Gold Camp Road. Either Bear Creek Road or Gold Camp Road can be used. They rejoin in another 1.1 miles at the exit end of High Drive. Continue 4.6 miles on the Gold Camp Road toward North Cheyenne Canyon to the parking area and the beginning of High Drive.

This parking area is the trailhead for Saint Mary's Falls and Seven Bridges Trails. Continue on the High Drive Road to reach the Bear Creek trailhead.

BEAR CREEK TRAIL #666

General description: A trail in Bear Canyon featuring a waterfall and fishing.

Elevation gain from Bear Creek trailhead to Jones Park Trail #667: 1,400'

Elevations: Highest: 8,500'   Lowest: 7,100'

Miles (round trip): 4

Rating: Easy

USGS topo map: Manitou Springs

Users: Mountain bikers, hikers

More road directions: The first mile of High Drive climbs steeply where it tops out at trailhead parking (Captain Jack's) for the Penrose

Multi-Use Trail #665 (upper end) to the right (east) and Jones Park Trail (formerly Buckhorn Trail) #667 to the left (west). If you reached the entrance to High Drive via the Gold Camp Road you would have passed the lower end of the **Penrose Trail** just before the first tunnel, at Mile 2.9 along the Gold Camp Road from the exit of High Drive. The Penrose Trail offers nice views of Colorado Springs. **Jones Park Trail #667** intersects with Bear Creek Trail #666 after 2.0 miles. If two cars are available, a one-way hike is possible using Bear Creek and Jones Park Trails. Jones Park and Penrose Trails are multi-use trails for motorcyclists, mountain bikers, horses, and hikers.

From this saddle, High Drive drops for 1.5 miles using switchbacks to reach the Bear Creek trailhead. The trailhead parking is located on one of these switchbacks.

Bear Creek Trail #666 begins along the creek, crossing it twice on log bridges within the first 0.25 mile. Several side trails leave the main trail in the first 0.3 mile, offering additional exploring, access to fishing, and a nice picnic spot. Just after the crossings the trail leaves the creek as it climbs high above. The trail continues above the creek for more than a mile, with views of a waterfall. The trail and creek come together again at the top of the waterfall. From here it is another 0.5 mile along the creek to its intersection with Jones Park Trail #667. Some sections of the trail are steep and gravelly.

Bear Creek Trail #666 ends at this junction, but by studying the maps and exploring on your own, you can make some very long, difficult hikes in this area. For example, you can follow Jones Park Trail 1.0 mile west to Jones Park. At the east end of Jones Park is Pipeline Trail #668. You can follow #668 to the Seven Bridges Spur #622A, which leads to Seven Bridges Trail #622. Seven Bridges Trail can be hiked to the parking area at the entrance to High Drive above Helen Hunt Falls. It would be wise to have a car in this parking lot as you'll lose 1,600' elevation. Getting back to your car at the Bear Creek trailhead could be exhausting.

Another option from the end of Bear Creek Trail is to follow Jones Park Trail west to the trail junction at the northwest end of Jones Park. Take the right fork (north) to climb Mount Garfield (see "Seven Bridges Trail" section).

A less exhausting option in conjunction with the Bear Creek Trail is to hike the Jones Park Trail 2.0 miles east (left fork) to Captain Jack's parking area on High Drive, where hopefully you've left a car. You can climb Mount Buckhorn as a side trip off this section of the Jones Park Trail. Its summit has some gigantic boulders.

SAINT MARY'S FALLS TRAIL #624

General description: A trail, partially along the old Gold Camp Road, that becomes rather steep near this beautiful cascade.

Rating: Moderate

USGS topo map: Manitou Springs

Users: Hikers

Option #1: *Elevation gain from parking area to base of Saint Mary's Falls:* 1,300'

Elevations: Highest: 8,800' Lowest: 7,500'

Miles (one way): 2.8

Option #2: *Elevation gain from parking area to top of Saint Mary's Falls via loop:* 1,800'

Elevations: Highest: 9,300' Lowest: 7,500'

Miles (round trip with loop at falls): 6.8

The collapse of a tunnel on the Gold Camp Road has made the hike to **Saint Mary's Falls** considerably longer than in the past. You must now park at the intersection of High Drive and Gold Camp Road above Helen Hunt Falls.

Saint Mary's Falls is a beautiful cascade that boils over rocks below the top of Stove Mountain. The trails at the falls have overlooks of the blue spruce and pine tree valley below, and of Colorado Springs.

From the parking area, hike 0.7 mile on the old Gold Camp Road to the road crossing of North Cheyenne Creek. Just before this creek crossing is the beginning of the Seven Bridges Trail (see "Seven Bridges Trail" section). Cross the creek, staying on the road for another 0.5 mile to the collapsed tunnel. Follow the trail to the top of the tunnel where the trail splits. Saint Mary's Falls Trail is the right fork. The left fork returns to the road, where you can pick up a trail along Buffalo Creek that shortly leads to the main Saint Mary's Falls Trail. The trail begins rather moderately as it follows along Buffalo Creek. If you've followed the main trail from the top of the tunnel, a trail split occurs after 0.1 mile. Either trail can be taken. As you continue, side trails lead to the creek.

The upper end of the trail becomes quite steep. There are two switchbacks before a trail junction sign. The sign says "St. Mary's Falls 500 feet," pointing left, and "Top of Falls 0.2 mile," pointing right. Either way, the sign is inaccurate about the distance. The base of the falls on the trail to the left is about 0.25 mile. The trail to the right reaches the top of the falls after a dozen switchbacks and a 1.0-mile hike. Don't plan to see the top of the falls when the trail finally reaches the top of the switchbacks and turns south towards the creek. This trail intersects another trail. The new trail, continued upstream (right), leads to Mount Rosa. If this trail is taken downstream (left) it will lead to the top of the falls. It's a very steep scramble on loose dirt and rock to return to the base of the falls via this trail. There are some nice views of the falls along this trail, but great care must be taken to avoid kicking rocks onto people who might be below at the base of the falls.

SEVEN BRIDGES TRAIL (NORTH CHEYENNE TRAIL) #622

General description: A trail, partially along the old Gold Camp Road, that meanders across North Cheyenne Creek with the aid of six bridges and, in conjunction with other area trails, offers a variety of outings.

Option #1: *Elevation gain to junction of Seven Bridges Trail and Seven Bridges Spur:* 1,300'

> *Elevations:* Highest: 8,800'   Lowest (at parking area): 7,500'
>
> *Miles (one way from parking area):* 2.2
>
> *Rating (Seven Bridges Trail only):* Easy
>
> *USGS topo map:* Manitou Springs
>
> *Users:* Horses, mountain bikers, hikers

Option #2: *Elevation gain, Seven Bridges Trail, Seven Bridges Spur, Jones Park Trail, and Mount Buckhorn Cutoff Trail loop (no side trips):* 1,760'

> *Miles (loop with no side trips):* 7
>
> *Rating:* Moderate

Statistics for trail segments:
Elevation gain, Seven Bridges Spur: 280'
  Highest elevation: 9,080'
  Lowest elevation: 8,800'
  Miles (one way): 0.5

Elevation gain from junction of Pipeline Trail and Jones Park Trail to Mount Garfield: 1,880'
  Highest elevation: 10,920'
  Lowest elevation: 9,040'
  Miles (one way): 1.5

Elevation loss from junction of Pipeline Trail and Jones Park Trail to junction of Jones Park Trail and Bear Creek Trail: 540'
  Highest elevation: 9,040'
  Lowest elevation: 8,500'
  Miles (one way): 1.0

Elevation gain from junction of Jones Park Trail and Bear Creek Trail to highest point on ridge to junction of Jones Park Trail and Mount Buckhorn Cutoff Trail: 180'
Elevation loss from highest point on ridge of Jones Park Trail to junction of Jones Park Trail and Mount Buckhorn Cutoff Trail: 480'
  Highest elevation: 8,680'
  Lowest elevation: 8,200'
  Miles (one way): 1.25

Elevation loss from junction of Jones Park Trail and Mount Buckhorn Cutoff Trail to junction of Mount Buckhorn Cutoff Trail and Seven Bridges Trail: 500'
  Highest elevation: 8,200'
  Lowest elevation: 7,700'
  Miles (one way): 1.25

Elevation loss from junction of Mount Buckhorn Cutoff Trail and Seven Bridges Trail to parking area at High Drive and Gold Camp Road intersection: 200'
  Highest elevation: 7,700'
  Lowest elevation: 7,500'
  Miles (one way): 0.8

Seven Bridges Trail begins on the old Gold Camp Road at the intersection of High Drive and Gold Camp Road above Helen Hunt Falls. The old Gold Camp Road has been blocked to vehicle traffic at the parking lot due to a tunnel collapse. Hike 0.7 mile down the road, leaving the road just before it crosses North Cheyenne Creek. The Mount Buckhorn Cutoff Trail comes in from the right 0.1 mile after leaving the road.

Despite its name, the main trail uses only six bridges. Shortly after the second bridge where the trail begins to turn south, the trail splits. You do not want to take the left fork over the third bridge because this trail quickly deteriorates. Stay on the right fork to the fourth bridge (third creek crossing). The trail to the last bridge is easy and very pleasant as it wanders back and forth over North Cheyenne Creek. Beyond the last bridge the trail becomes much steeper. When the trail reaches an open gravelly slope it splits. Taking the higher trail through this area saves a rather steep bushwhack up the hill to regain the main trail. In 1.5 miles after leaving the road, Seven Bridges Trail reaches a trail junction and a tributary that comes in from the north (right). Seven Bridges Trail (straight ahead) crosses the tributary and continues a short distance to its end at Pipeline Trail #668.

Instead of retracing your steps from this point, a nice option is to hike the right fork up the tributary on the Seven Bridges Spur #622A (formerly North Cheyenne Cutoff). You can then climb Mount Garfield or make a loop trip. A few yards up the spur, the trail splits and follows both sides of the tributary. Stay on the east side of the creek. After another 0.1 mile from the trail split, the trail becomes faint in a grassy aspen meadow. Continue along the creek, noting when the creek changes direction to come from the west. The two trails rejoin here on the north (right) side of the creek. At this junction the trail turns abruptly north. After a few feet there is another junction. Take the right fork, which leaves the creek and climbs to the saddle west of Kineo Mountain. After a 280'-elevation gain from the Seven Bridges Trail and a short walk across the saddle, the trail starts down and ends at Mile 0.5 on the Pipeline Trail #668. Turn right (north) and follow #668 0.1 mile down to Bear Creek, which must be crossed without aid of a bridge. Trail #668 intersects Jones Park Trail #667 just after the creek crossing.

If climbing Mount Garfield is your destination, turn left (west) on Jones Park Trail #667 at the junction of #667 and #668. Hike 0.3 mile to the northwest end of Jones Park, where the trail forks. Take the right (north) fork for a three-minute walk to the remains of an old cabin. Note that the trail at the cabin crosses a small creek to the east side and continues up the gully. It's tempting to use this trail to climb Mount Garfield but it dead-ends about 0.4 mile beyond the cabin. To climb Mount Garfield, go to the west side of the cabin next to the hillside. A steep, eroded trail climbs up the hillside to a ridge. Follow the ridge to the top of Mount Garfield.

An old cabin at base of Mount Garfield—Seven Bridges and Jones Park Trails

If climbing Mount Garfield doesn't interest you, a loop trip can be made by turning east (right) at the junction of Trails #667 and #668 and continuing down Bear Canyon on the Jones Park Trail. About 0.3 mile down the Jones Park Trail from the junction of #667 and #668 is the entrance to an old mine. Use your own judgment about exploring it. Old mines can be very dangerous. From the junction of #667 and #668, it is 1.0 mile with a 540' elevation loss to the junction of Jones Park Trail #667 and Bear Creek Trail #666 (see "Bear Creek Trail" section).

The Jones Park Trail crosses Bear Creek at the Bear Creek Trail (straight ahead) and Jones Park Trail (right fork) junction. A log bridge, just a few feet below the main crossing, keeps your feet out of Bear Creek. After the creek crossing, Jones Park Trail climbs steeply in a short distance to the top of the ridge that separates the Bear Creek and North Cheyenne Creek drainages. Once on the ridge, the trail skirts to the north side of a high point. It then crosses over the ridge, makes a small switchback, and continues as a short but wonderful ridge walk to the low point on the ridge southwest of an 8,540' point. As the trail heads northeast toward Mount Buckhorn, it stays to the southeast side of the 8,540' point. A short bushwhack to the top of the 8,540' point gives a great view west-southwest to Kineo and Almagre Mountains, and into Bear Canyon.

The trail continues northeast to the saddle below Mount Buckhorn and the junction of Jones Park Trail and Mount Buckhorn Cutoff Trail. Mount Buckhorn can be climbed as a side trip from this junction by continuing 0.1 mile on the Jones Park Trail to a trail junction. The trail to the left (north) follows the ridge to Mount Buckhorn, which has some gigantic boulders. To complete the loop back to your car, retrace your steps to the saddle and take the Mount Buckhorn Cutoff Trail, which heads southwest (1.25 miles) to the Seven Bridges Trail. As you descend the cutoff trail you might be able to spot your car in the parking lot below.

Seven Bridges Trail and Seven Bridges Spur are non-motorized, but the Pipeline Trail, Jones Park Trail, and Mount Buckhorn Cutoff Trail will be shared with motorcycles. Mountain bikers and horse riders may be encountered on any of these trails.

WALDO CANYON TRAIL #640

General description: A popular trail with great views of Pikes Peak.

Elevation gain: 1,060'

Elevations: Highest: 8,080'   Lowest: 7,020'

Miles (round trip): 6.8

Rating: Easy to moderate

USGS topo map: Cascade

Users: Mountain bikers, hikers

Road directions: From I-25 take Exit 141 to Manitou Springs on US 24. The trailhead is located on US 24, two miles west of the exit to Cave of the Winds (or 7 miles from the junction of I-25 and US 24). There is a large parking area on the right side of the highway.

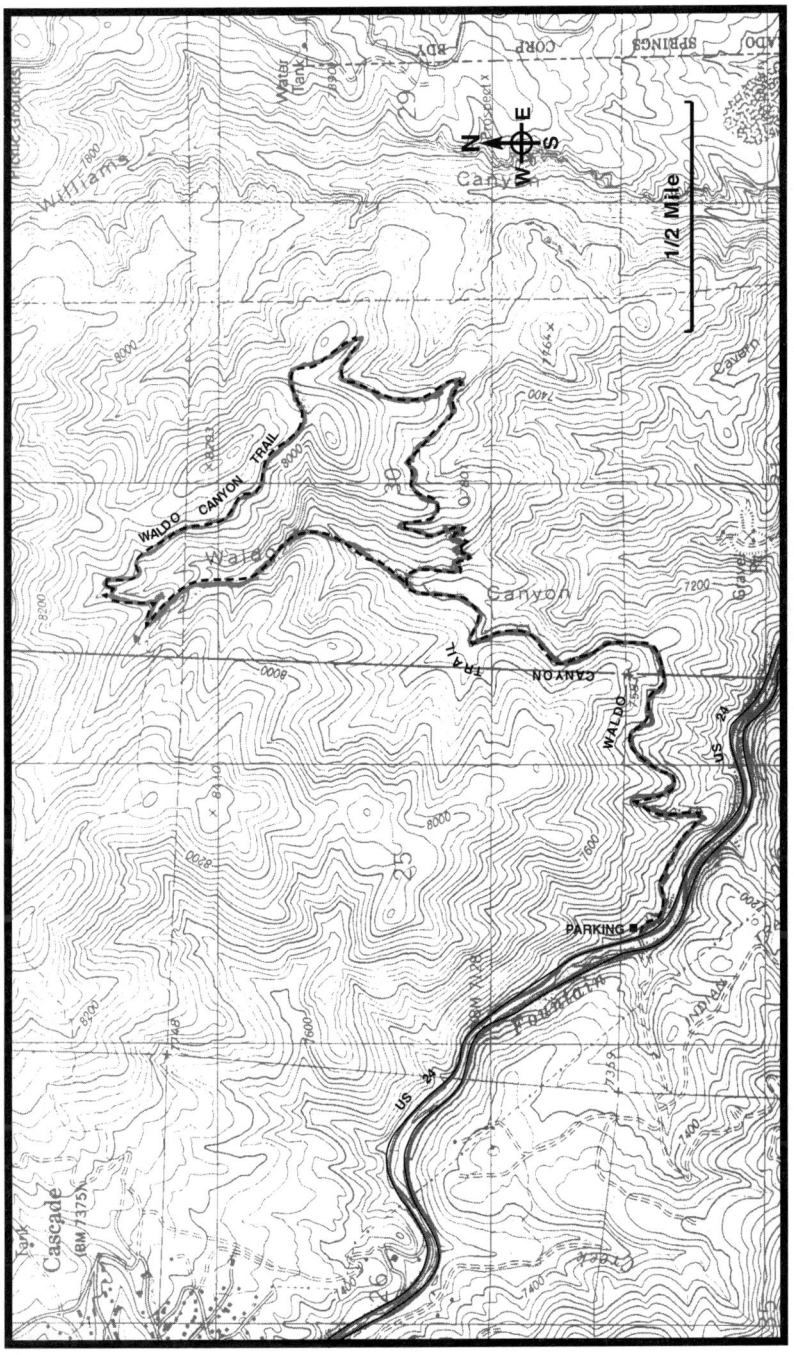

Waldo Canyon Trail initially parallels the highway before turning north and then east to gain access to Waldo Canyon. From the trailhead it is 1.6 miles to a meadow with a stream that is supposedly the former site of the Waldo Hog Ranch. At the north end of the meadow is the junction to the 3.5-mile loop section of the trail.

The loop section of the trail has many side trails that lead to rocky outcrops, ridges, and overlooks. The trail is easiest if hiked clockwise. From this junction (going clockwise) the trail climbs for a mile, up through the bottom of Waldo Canyon, crossing the creek several times before coming to a fork in the trail. The fork to the left (west) leads towards Cascade. If you follow this trail, it will stay in the canyon for about a mile before climbing to the top of a ridge. The trail along this ridge can then be followed back to the Waldo Canyon Trail, reaching it about 1.0 mile above the parking area. The ridge has some great views, but it also has some steep gravelly sections, which make a walking staff handy. If you do this loop, it's 6.5 miles.

If you are continuing on the more popular Waldo Canyon Trail, go right at the junction, where the trail continues the loop by doubling back on itself to gain the top of the ridge. After leaving the ridge, the trail crosses a small creek and then follows the slopes on the east side above the bottom of Waldo Canyon. A series of switchbacks near the end of the loop drop you back into the bottom of the canyon and to the beginning of the loop. You must then retrace your steps to the trailhead.

Red rock spires - Red Canyon Park, Canon City

Bullsnake - East Pierce Gulch Trail, Canon City

Sunflowers - Fremont Peak Trail, Canon City

Red Columbine - Newlin Creek Trail, Florence / Wetmore

Steam Engine - Newlin Creek Trail, Florence / Wetmore

Poison ivy in autumn

Arkansas River in winter - Conduit Nature Trail, Pueblo

Apache Falls in winter - Apache Falls Trail, Rye

Fog and fall - Bartlett Trail, Rye

Marion Lake in September - Saint Charles Trail, San Isabel

Natural Arch on Little Saint Charles Creek
San Carlos Trail, San Isabel

Marion Mine - Marion Mine Trail, San Isabel

FLORENCE AREA

NEWLIN CREEK TRAIL #1335

General description: A favorite hike that features waterfalls, rocky cliffs, and an old steam engine.

Elevation gain: 1,460'

Elevations: Highest: 8,360' Lowest: 6,900'

Miles (round trip from 0.2 mile below pond): 6

Rating: Easy

USGS topo map: Rockvale

Users: Hikers

Road directions: From the junction of CO 115 and CO 67 in Florence, drive south on CO 67 for 4.3 miles to Fremont County Road 15. Or from the junction of CO 96 and CO 67 in Wetmore, drive north on CO 67 for 6.8 miles to Fremont County Road 15. Follow County Road 15 in a southwest direction. At Mile 5.6 there is a fence line with an open gate and a Florence Mountain Park sign. Just inside the gate, continue straight ahead at the junction (do not go up the hill to the right). At Mile 5.8 the road to the left goes to Florence Mountain Park. Continue straight ahead at this fork for 0.1 mile to a private residence. Please respect the private property. Parking is available 0.2 mile beyond the house. Or, if the road is not too badly washed out, continue for another 0.2 mile to a small dam and pond at the trailhead. There are two small parking areas at the pond.

The pond and the dam at the **Newlin Creek Trailhead** have undergone several renovations over the years, but historical evidence indicates that they were first built for the coal mining industry in the early 1900s. A series of small, picturesque waterfalls along Newlin Creek make this trail especially delightful in the spring. Even if the waterfalls are just a trickle, they add beauty to the rocky cliffs that loom above the creek.

At the end of the trail is a beautiful meadow, complete with an old steam engine. The steam-powered sawmill was apparently established by Nathaniel F. Herrick in 1887. The intent seemed to be to provide lumber for the coal mining towns in the Coal Creek area and for the silver mining camps in the Silver Cliff vicinity. But

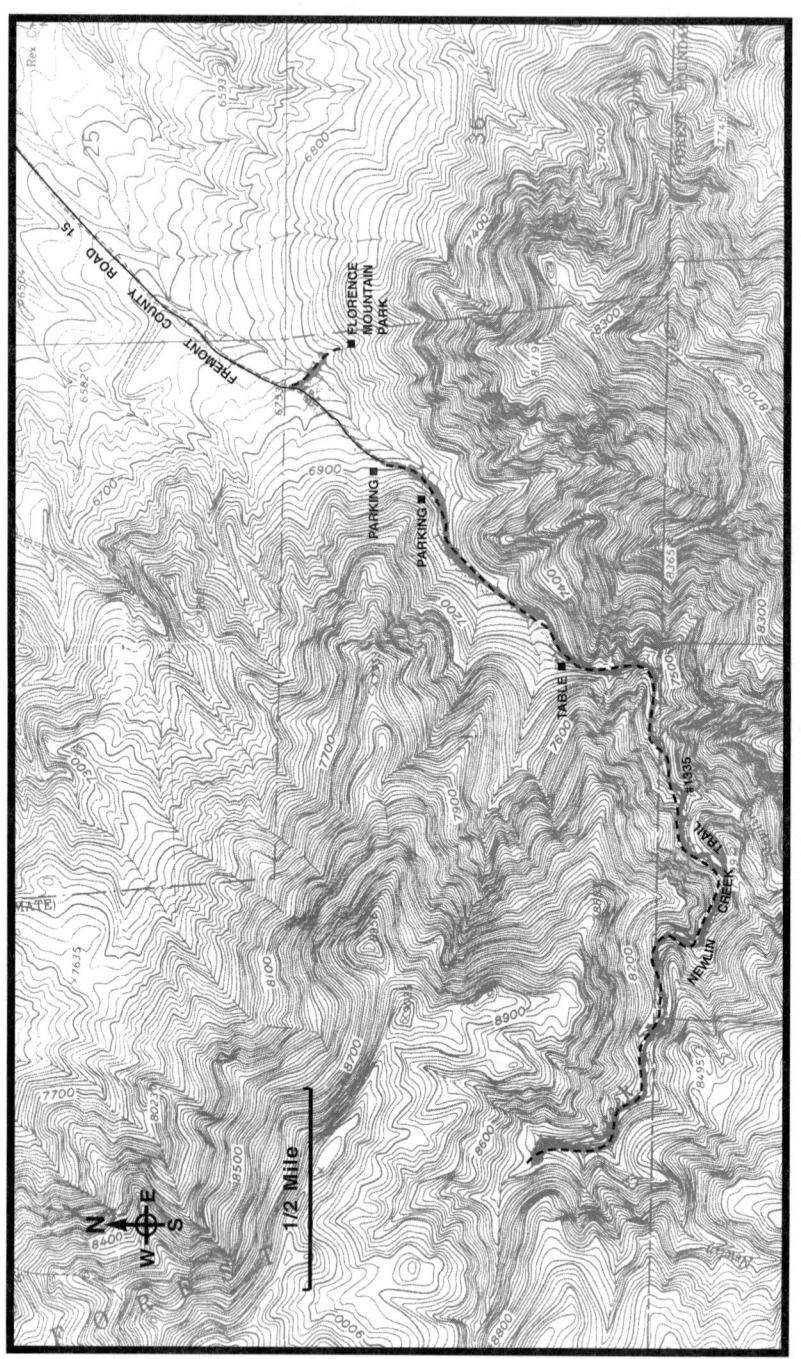

Waterfall—Newlin Creek Trail

Herrick died in that same year, resulting in abandonment of the project. The road washed out, making it too costly to remove the steam engine.

The trail follows the remnants of the old wagon and logging road, past a picnic table, to the end of the road at a bridge crossing 0.6 mile from the pond. The bridge crossing is the first of 17 crossings of Newlin Creek. It is the only bridge, so enjoy it! The trail also crosses a few side creeks, the largest being South Newlin Creek at Mile 1.25 from the pond. Two side creeks (one may be dry) will be crossed near the end of the trail. The creek crossings will slow you down a bit, but a few appropriately placed logs and rocks help ease the way.

The meadow is a great place to eat lunch, to inspect the steam engine, and to ponder Colorado's history. Please do not vandalize or remove any of these historic structures. Leave this piece of history for others to enjoy.

OPHIR CREEK—BIGELOW DIVIDE (FAIRVIEW) AREA

TRAILS FROM DITCH CREEK ROAD

Road directions: The Ditch Creek Road (Forest Road 383) on CO 165 can be reached in two ways and gives access to the **Left Hand Fork Trail** (formerly the North Creek Trail) and **Silver Circle Trail**. From San Isabel, drive north on CO 165 for 9.6 miles; or from McKenzie Junction at CO 165 and CO 96, drive south on CO 165 for 8.9 miles. Ditch Creek Road is passable for all cars for the first mile, but deteriorates quickly to high-clearance vehicles only. Parking is available for low-clearance vehicles at 1.0 mile, where the road makes a 90-degree turn to the right. The road forks immediately after the sharp corner. Take the lower right fork. Before the next junction you will pass the Mingus Ranch homestead site. You may wish to stop and read the historical signs provided by the Forest Service. At the next junction, go straight ahead on Forest Road 383A for 0.2 mile to trailhead parking for Left Hand Fork Trail, or turn right to continue on Forest Road 383 to the Silver Circle trailhead parking. From CO 165, the Left Hand Fork trailhead is 2.0 miles and the Silver Circle trailhead is 3.6 miles.

LEFT HAND FORK TRAIL #1325

General description: A trail with many wildflowers that descends to private property.

Elevation loss (regained on return trip): 1,800'

Elevations: Highest: 9,200'   Lowest: 7,400'

Miles (round trip): 5.5

Rating: Moderate

USGS topo map: Saint Charles Peak

Users: Hikers

The **Left Hand Fork Trail** descends 2.0 miles to private property. The trail can be hiked on private property another 0.75 mile before it becomes prudent to turn around. When hiking on private property please stay on the trail. Once off the ridge the trail follows creek beds, but take your own water supply. Wildflowers can be plentiful so take your flower identification guide. As you descend, remember not to hike farther down than you can safely climb back up. You may not be looked upon too kindly if you have to seek help from the ranchers on the North Creek Road.

SILVER CIRCLE TRAIL #1323

General description: Features ruins in the Silver Circle meadow, access to the Middle Creek Trail, and access to the Scraggy Peaks.

Elevation loss (regained on return trip): 1,900'

Elevations: Highest: 9,500'   Lowest (at private property): 7,600'

Miles (round trip to private property): 8

Rating: Moderate

USGS topo map: Saint Charles Peak

Users: Motorcyclists, horses, hikers

The **Silver Circle Trail** immediately begins descending to the Silver Circle meadow (Mile 1.25) and to the ruins of three cabins. Hike through the meadow, past the ruins, to a junction and sign. The

Looking east in Silver Circle meadow—Silver Circle Trail

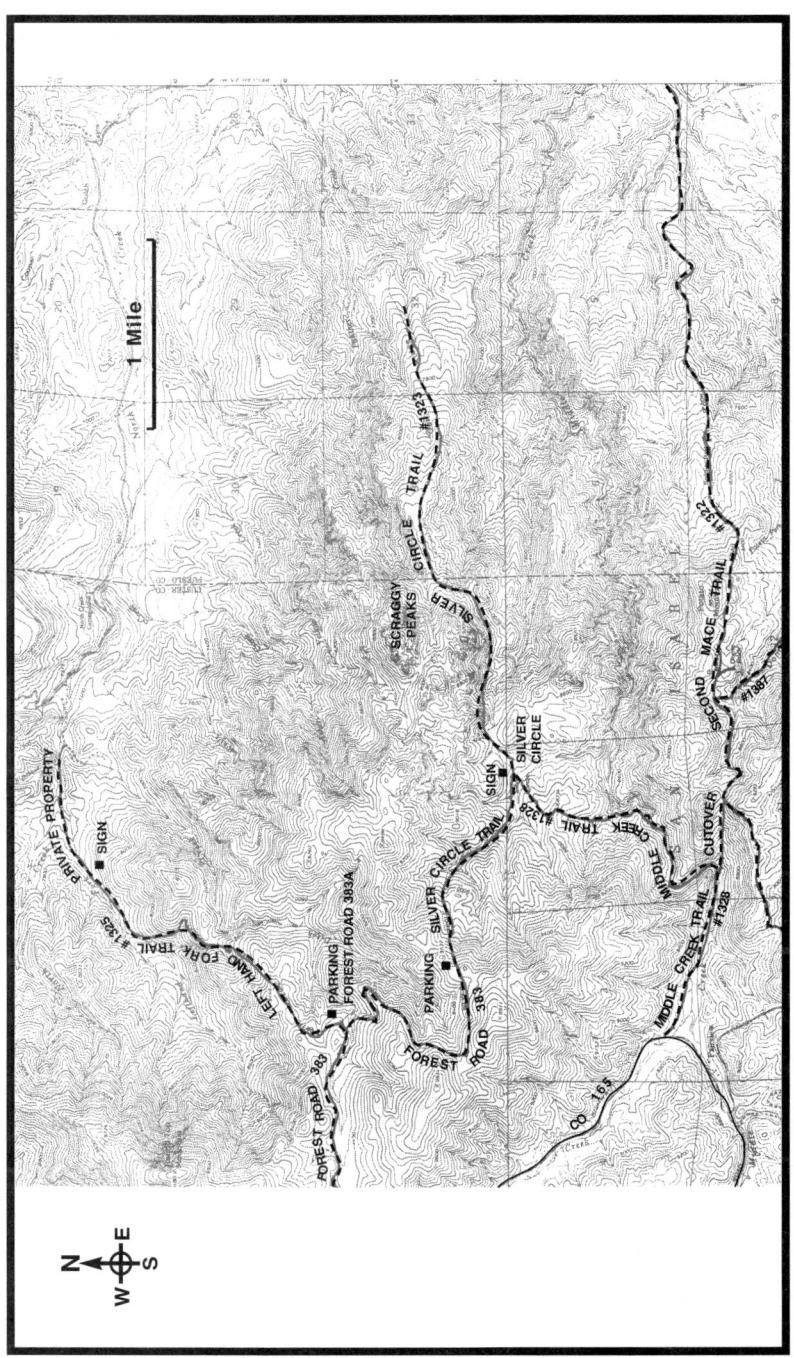

right fork (south) leads to Middle Creek in 1.0 mile on the Middle Creek Trail (see "Middle Creek Trail" section). The left fork (east-northeast) is a continuation of the Silver Circle Trail and will take you past the Scraggy Peaks and down Oak Ridge.

The Scraggy Peaks are fun to explore, but they are very rugged and no trail penetrates them. A good place to begin your exploration is at about Mile 2.5 (8,400') at the east end of the peaks.

Scraggy Peaks—Silver Circle Trail

Leaving the peaks, the trail continues descending along Oak Ridge, where it ends at about 7,600' elevation on private property, 4.0 miles from the trailhead.

The streams along the trail are delightful in spring runoff, but always take plenty of water from home for that uphill return to your vehicle.

SECOND MACE TRAIL #1322

General description: A pleasant descent to Soldier Park (and return), and access to Middle Creek and Dome Rock Trails.

Elevation gain from CO 165: 320'

Elevation gain from Davenport Campground: 560'

Elevation loss, Second Mace and Second Mace Cutover Trails junction to Beulah: 2,580'

Elevations: Highest from CO 165: 9,200'
Lowest (Vine Mesa Avenue parking): 6,500'
Elevation at Second Mace and Second Mace Cutover Trails junction: 9,080'

Miles (CO 165 to Beulah—one way): 6.75

Rating: Moderate

USGS topo maps: Beulah, Saint Charles Peak

Users: Motorcyclists (west end), horses, hikers

Road directions: The west end of the Second Mace Trail is on CO 165 and the east end is in Beulah. See "Beulah Area: Second Mace Trail" section for road directions and for concerns about the east end of the trail. The Second Mace Trail begins on CO 165 at Bishop Castle, 5.7 miles north of San Isabel. However, to avoid highway parking and congestion at Bishop Castle, you may wish to use the Second Mace Cutover Trail at Davenport Campground. If you're making a loop trip using the Squirrel Creek and Dome Rock Trails (see "Beulah Area" section), you may also wish to park at this trailhead. To reach the cutover trailhead, drive 5.3 miles north of San Isabel on CO 165 to the Davenport Campground turnoff (Forest Road 382). The trailhead is 1.25 miles down the Davenport Campground road. The Squirrel Creek trailhead is another 0.25 mile at the end of the campground road.

From CO 165, the **Second Mace Trail** begins steeply, climbing 200' to cross a saddle at 0.5 mile. It then turns north for a short distance, descending 240', then regains 120'. A mile from the trailhead on CO 165, you reach a trail junction. The trail coming from the south (right) is the Second Mace Cutover Trail from the Davenport Campground. The main disadvantage of the cutover trail is that it requires an elevation gain of 560' versus 320'. The cutover trail to the junction with the Second Mace Trail is also 1.0 mile.

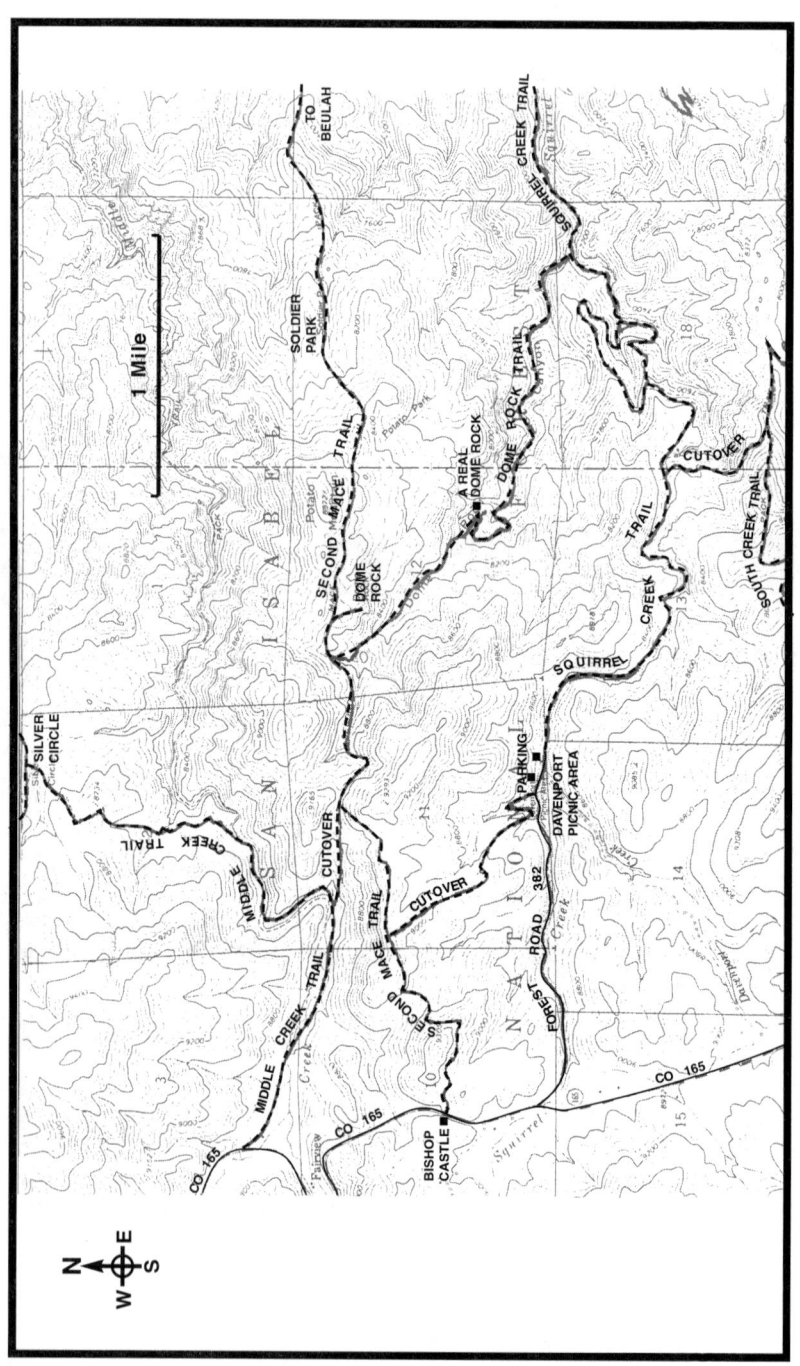

Heading east from the Second Mace/Cutover Trail junction toward Beulah, in another long 0.5 mile, is a second trail junction at a saddle. The trail, which heads west as it leaves the Second Mace Trail (north side), descends to the Middle Creek Trail (see "Middle Creek Trail" section).

After 2.25 miles from either the CO 165 trailhead or the Davenport Campground trailhead, you'll come to the junction with Dome Rock Trail #1387. Take the right fork if you're making a loop using Dome Rock and Squirrel Creek Trails.

If you continue on the Second Mace Trail you'll pass Dome Rock, which is to the south (0.1 mile from the junction), and then Potato Mountain, which is to the north (0.6 mile from the junction and not very obvious). As you continue your hike to Beulah you'll pass through Soldier Park at Mile 3.5 from CO 165. If you've hiked this trail from Beulah to Soldier Park, you'll recognize two huge white fir trees growing at the west edge of this open meadow. A dead tree is squeezed between the two firs.

If you're making a one-way trip from Soldier Park, it is 2.75 miles to the trailhead in Beulah, plus another 0.5 mile on the road to your car parked outside the gate on Vine Mesa Avenue. Some sections of the trail are steep.

MIDDLE CREEK TRAIL #1328

General description: Serves primarily as a link between the Second Mace Trail and the Silver Circle Trail, but has a spur that leads to CO 165.

Elevation gain from Second Mace Trail to sign at Silver Circle meadow: 280'

Elevation gain from sign at Silver Circle meadow to Second Mace Trail: 800'

Elevation loss from CO 165 at spur trailhead to lowest elevation on Middle Creek: 240'

Highest elevation (at saddle on Second Mace Trail): 9,000'

Highest elevation (Middle Creek to sign at Silver Circle meadow): 8,720'

Lowest elevation (along Middle Creek): 8,440'

Elevation at sign at Silver Circle meadow: 8,480'

White fir trees in Soldier Park—Second Mace Trail

Elevation at CO 165 spur trailhead: 8,680'

Miles (from Second Mace Trail to sign at Silver Circle meadow—one way): 2.25

Miles (spur trail only—one way): 1

Rating: Easy

USGS topo map: Saint Charles Peak

Users: Motorcyclists and horses (but not on spur), hikers

Road directions: Refer to the road directions for the Second Mace Trail at Bishop Castle and the Silver Circle Trail. To reach the spur trailhead, drive 1.5 miles north of Bishop Castle (0.6 mile beyond the Ophir Creek Road turnoff) on CO 165 to an old homestead on the east side of the highway. Parking is limited because you need to park outside the gate along the highway.

To hike the **Middle Creek Trail** from the spur trailhead go through the gate, closing it behind you. Follow the trail east past the homestead buildings. The trail crosses Middle Creek to the south side in 0.5 mile, where it stays to its junction with the side trail coming from the Second Mace Trail. Note that toward the east end of the meadow at a fence line the trail becomes very overgrown, so once through the fence line stay close to the trees on the south edge of the meadow until you reach the side trail junction and signs. At the junction, the trail up the hill leads to the Second Mace Trail. Continue straight ahead on the Middle Creek Trail to the Silver Circle meadow. The spur trail is 1.0 mile through private property.

If you've started from the Second Mace trailhead at Bishop Castle, hike a long 1.5 miles to a saddle and the junction with a side trail that descends west from the saddle to Middle Creek. When the side trail reaches the meadow at the bottom of the hill, turn right (east). The trail follows Middle Creek for 0.75 mile, crossing it once, before turning north toward the Silver Circle meadow. In the next 1.0 mile from Middle Creek, the trail crosses several ridges before making its final descent to the sign at the east end of the Silver Circle meadow. From the meadow you can hike west 1.5 miles on the Silver Circle Trail to Forest Road 383, or hike east past the Scraggy Peaks and down Oak Ridge.

SAINT CHARLES TRAIL FROM OPHIR CREEK ROAD

General description: An easy way to climb Saint Charles Peak.

Elevation gain to peak: 304'

Elevations: Highest: 11,784' Elevation at trailhead: 11,520'

Miles (round trip to peak): 1.2

Rating: Easy

USGS topo maps: Deer Peak, Saint Charles Peak

Users: Motorcyclists, hikers

Road directions: The Saint Charles Trail can be reached from the west side of Saint Charles Peak. It is more than a 50-mile drive from Pueblo, but is included for your information. From San Isabel, drive 6.7 miles north on CO 165 to the Ophir Creek Road (Forest Road 360) at Fairview. Drive 8.2 miles up the Ophir Creek Road to Promontory Divide, where Forest Road 360 ends. Take Forest Road 369 (Greenhorn Mountain Road) for 2.0 miles to Forest Road 335. Follow Forest Road 335 (high-clearance vehicles only) for 2.0 miles to its end and the parking area for the Saint Charles Trail.

To climb Saint Charles Peak from the parking area at the end of Forest Road 335, continue southeast on the faint road to the sign that directs you to the trail. You'll have to descend about 40' and 0.1 mile to pick up the **Saint Charles Trail**. Once at the Saint Charles Trail, turn left (west-northwest) to cross over a low ridge before turning north to the peak. Saint Charles Peak (11,784') is 0.5 mile from the junction of the access trail and Saint Charles Trail. You'll have to leave the main trail to reach the top of the peak. Reference the "San Isabel Area" section for more details on the Saint Charles Trail.

PENROSE AREA

AIKEN CANYON PRESERVE

General description: A popular birding area with pretty scenery and some historical structures.

Elevation gain with side trail: 920'

Elevations: Highest at end of side trail: 7,400'   Lowest: 6,480'

Miles in preserve: 4.25

Rating: Easy

USGS topo maps: Mount Big Chief, Mount Pittsburg

Users: Hikers

Road directions: From the junction of US 50 and CO 115 at Penrose, drive north on CO 115 17.9 miles (or 4.7 miles north of the Fremont/El Paso County line) to the Turkey Canyon Ranch Road. Turn left (west) onto the road and drive 0.2 mile to the parking area, which is on the right.

The **Aiken Canyon Preserve** is home to an abundant amount of wildlife. To protect the wildlife, it is open to foot traffic only. No pets are allowed. The area is open from dawn to dusk on Saturday, Sunday, and Monday year-round. Binoculars are helpful for observing the many birds. A good place to start your visit is at the Nature Conservancy Field Station if it is open. The Preserve is named after ornithologist Charles Aiken, who lived in Turkey Creek Canyon. The trail is well marked and easy to follow. The map shows the approximate location of the trail. Please stay on the trail to protect this area.

The 1,621-acre preserve is located between the mountains of the Beaver Creek Wilderness Study Area to the west and the plains of the Fort Carson Military Reservation to the east, and serves as a corridor for many animal species. Wildlife includes rodents, bobcat, mountain lion, badger, coyote, gray fox, mule deer, elk, and black bear. Over 100 species of birds have been documented in Aiken Canyon, including prairie falcon, golden eagle, red-tailed hawk, wild turkey, scrub jay, Virginia's warbler, western tanager, western bluebird, hairy and downy woodpecker, and Townsend's solitaire. The lower elevations have gambel oak, one-seeded juniper, piñon pine, yucca, cactus, and

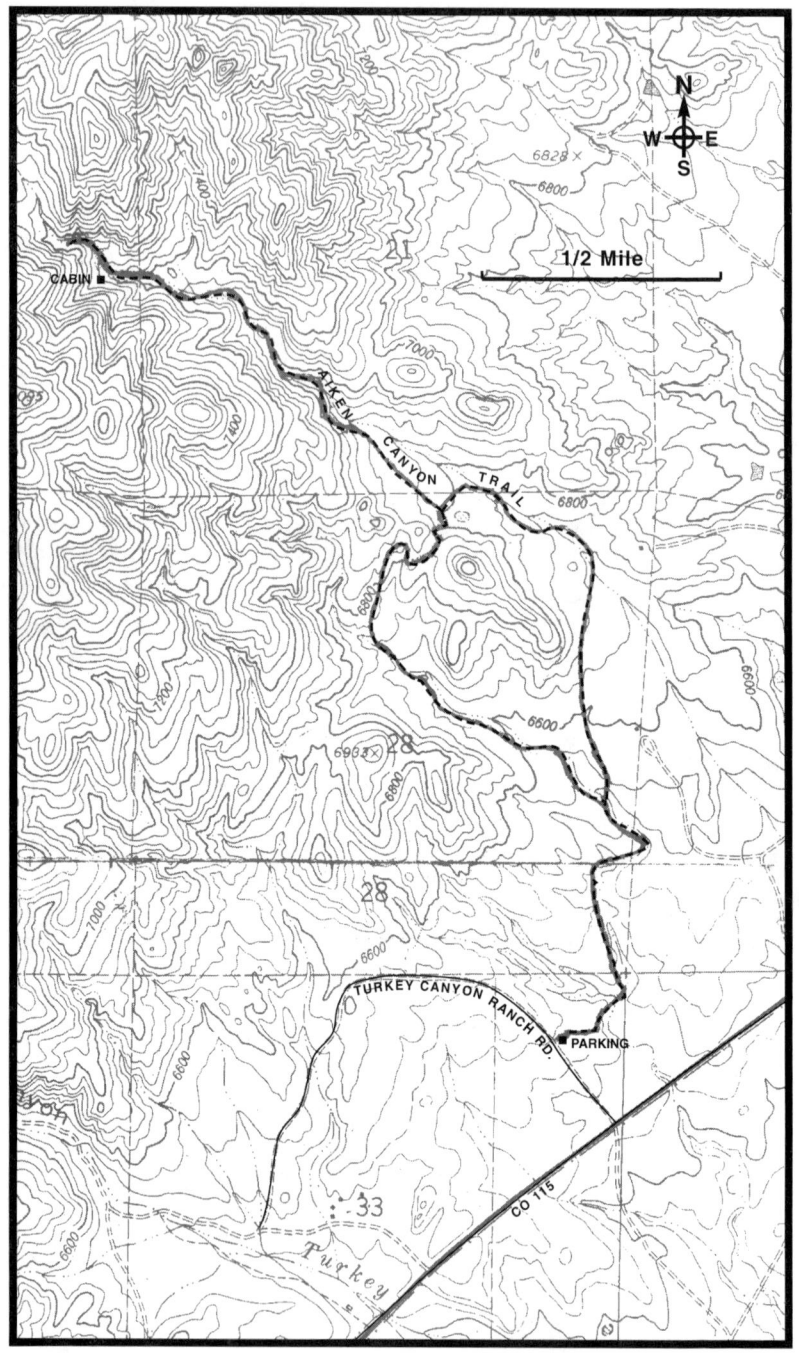

open meadows. The higher elevations have old growth ponderosa pine and white fir. The Nature Conservancy rescued the area from gravel mining, but housing development still encroaches on the area. But hopefully, Aiken Canyon Preserve will be a wildlife sanctuary for years to come.

A 4-mile loop trail begins as a single trail but splits in about 0.75 mile. Take the time to read the eight informational signs along this 0.75-mile section of the trail. It is best to do the loop counter-clockwise. Going right at the junction is a more gradual climb. Near the top end of the loop, the trail begins to head westerly to circumvent a large knoll before turning south. About 0.1 mile after turning south, there is a trail junction at the base of the knoll. This is about the halfway point if you are just doing the loop. The trail to the right (northwest) leads to the remnants of an old cabin in 1.0 mile and is worth the hike into the huge old pine trees. An "End of Trail" sign is at a waterfall just above the cabin. Retrace your steps to the junction. From this junction continue south, going up a couple of switchbacks as you pass the large knoll that you have been hiking around. As you begin your descent, there is a nice view of the Spanish Peaks and Greenhorn Mountain to the south.

TRAILS FROM UPPER BEAVER CREEK ROAD (FREMONT COUNTY ROAD 132)

Road directions: **Beaver Creek Trail** and **Trail Gulch Trail** begin as the same trail at the end of the Upper Beaver Creek Road. To reach the Upper Beaver Creek Road, drive west on US 50 4.2 miles from the junction of US 50 and CO 115 at Penrose (26.5 miles from the junction of Pueblo Boulevard and US 50) to the exit for Victor, Cripple Creek, and Brush Hollow Reservoir (CO 67). There is a traffic light at the junction of US 50 and CO 67. Drive north on CO 67 (also known as Phantom Canyon Road) 1.7 miles to Fremont County Road 123. Turn right (east) and drive 0.3 mile to Fremont County Road 132. Turn north onto Fremont County Road 132 (Upper Beaver Creek Road). Continue 10.8 miles to the parking area and the trailhead. The last 4 or 5 miles of this road can be quite muddy when wet, requiring a 4-wheel-drive vehicle.

Overview: The 27,020-acre Beaver Creek Wilderness Study Area is rugged and beautiful. It is home to beaver, Rocky Mountain bighorn sheep, mule deer, elk, bobcat, mountain lion, and black bear. Hawks, eagles, and peregrine falcons may soar through the skies. The hillsides are graced with juniper, pine, fir, and spruce. Rocks include granites, gneisses, and schists. Mica along the trail is dazzling.

A nice loop trip can be made by using the Beaver Creek Trail, the connecting Power Line (Pole) Trail, and Trail Gulch Trail. Because of a rocky cliff along Beaver Creek and the steepness of the Power Line Trail, the loop trip is not recommended for horses. Because this is a wilderness study area, motorized vehicles and mountain bikes are not allowed. Poison ivy is prevalent.

BEAVER CREEK TRAIL

General description: A rolling trail with accesses to a fishermen's creek in the rugged and beautiful Beaver Creek Wilderness Study Area.

Elevation gain (loop): 1,400'

Elevations: Highest (loop): 7,500'   Lowest: 6,100'

Miles (round trip loop): 7

Rating: Moderate

USGS topo map: Phantom Canyon

Users: Backpackers, fishermen, hikers

Beaver Creek Trail begins as a road through a meadow at the end of the Upper Beaver Creek Road. At 0.1 mile from the trailhead, a road splitting off to the right leads to Banta Gulch. Stay to the left, where in 100 yards you'll cross a dry creek bed. At 0.3 mile from the trailhead is a second junction with a signless post. Either way works, but the route to the left is mostly a fishermen's access. If you go left, the road continues along Beaver Creek for 0.1 mile to a water control structure. In just a few more yards, the road crosses a spillway on a log footbridge at a small dam and becomes a trail. The trail continues between a ditch and Beaver Creek for 0.1 mile to another log footbridge. Cross the ditch and continue upstream for 50 feet, where you will find a steep path up the hillside. Since this path is so steep, it is best explored on the return trip. If you miss the path up the hill, you will soon find yourself at a dead end where the ditch siphons water from Beaver Creek. The path up the hillside joins the main trail at the top of the hill.

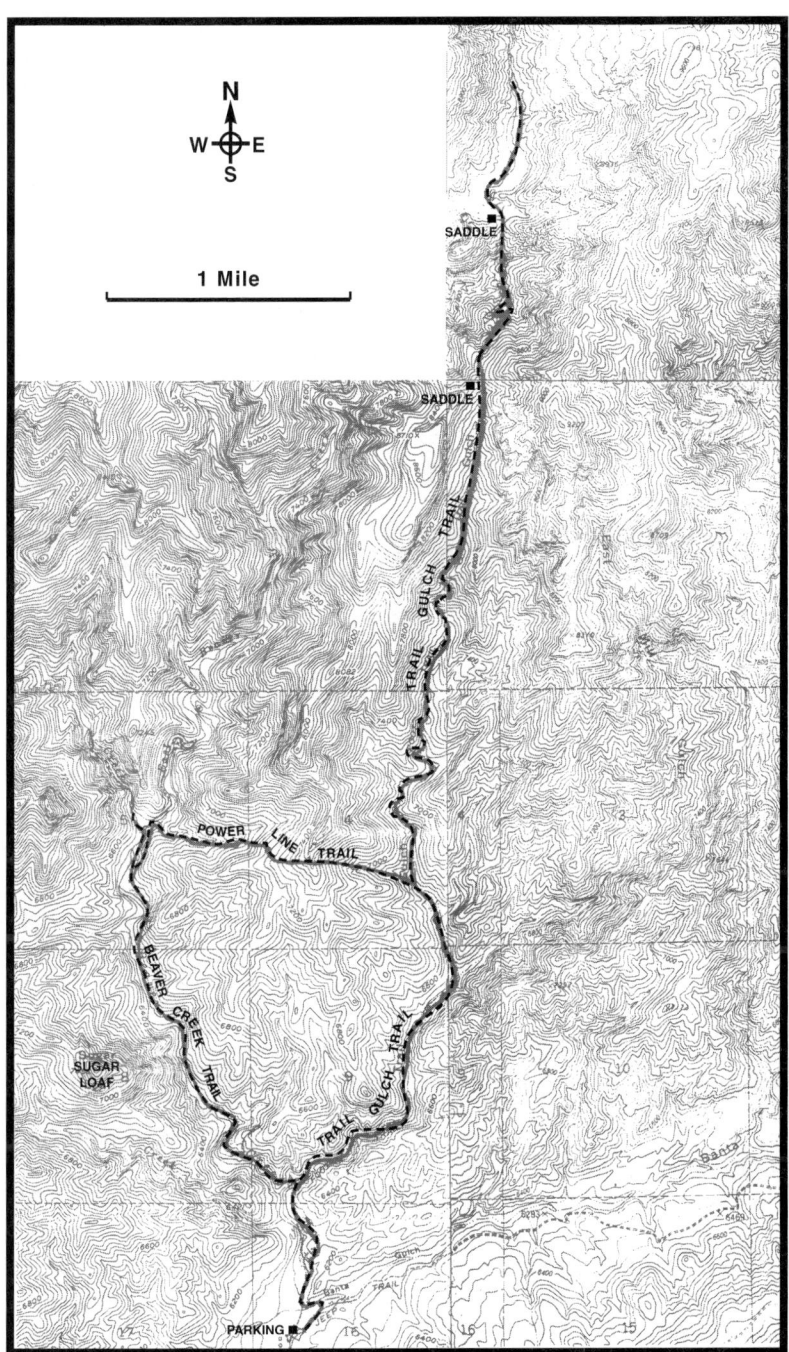

- 111 -

The trail to the right from the junction at the post goes up through a dry wash and in 0.25 mile forms yet another junction. A dry gulch and old road split off to the right. Notice the rocks that block off this road, which quickly dead-ends. Staying on the trail to the left leads in 0.2 mile to a gate arch and fence. There is no gate to open or close. About 70 yards on the north side of the gate opening will be the top end of the path mentioned above. Heading north from the gate, the trail descends in 0.1 mile to the junction of Beaver Creek Trail (left fork) and Trail Gulch Trail (right fork). This junction, marked by a cairn, is 0.8 mile from the trailhead.

Trailhead—Beaver Creek and Trail Gulch Trails

Beyond this junction, fishermen, hikers, and backpackers will find the rolling Beaver Creek Trail a delight as it snakes in and out of the gullies. However, several dead-end side trails, which sometimes look more traveled than the main trail, could cause some frustration.

The first problem dead-end side trail is about 0.3 mile after leaving the junction of Beaver Creek Trail and Trail Gulch Trail. The dead-end trail continues straight ahead but is blocked by logs. If you continue on this side trail it goes around a corner, then fades high above the creek. The main trail is more obscure and switches steeply down the hill to the left in 0.25 mile to Beaver Creek. Once at the creek, a rocky cliff along Beaver Creek and a side creek will force you to wade through Beaver Creek to get past these two obstacles.

The next difficult junction is about 1.0 mile north of the rocky cliff and side creek obstacles. Across Beaver Creek to the west, at this point, is a sizable canyon that is north of Sugar Loaf Mountain. The trail to the right is steep and goes to a nice overlook, but you want the trail to the left, which goes down to the creek. Once at the creek and a large cairn, do not cross the main creek. But instead, cross the outlet of a slough, which is alongside a rock wall. Once across the outlet, follow the path through the willows along the slough and rock wall.

At 0.25 mile farther north from the slough crossing, there is yet one more junction. If you plan to camp at the confluence of West and East Beaver Creeks, you might consider the left fork. If you don't mind more wading, a nice campsite is on the west side of Beaver Creek. For other campsites along East Beaver Creek, or if you're doing the loop over Power Line (Pole) Trail to Trail Gulch Trail, you'll want to take the route up the hill to the right. When you reach the trail junction that will take you east over the top of the ridge at 7,500' on Power Line Trail, note the overlook on a rocky outcrop and the relics from another time. You'll need to hunt in the oak brush for the start of the trail that takes you down to the campsites along East Beaver Creek.

From the confluence of West and East Beaver Creeks, you'll climb 900' in 1.0 mile on Power Line Trail to a ridge that gives some nice views of the Beaver Creek drainage. As you descend 800' in 0.7 mile (very steep) to Trail Gulch Trail, you'll see why the cutover trail is named Power Line (Pole) Trail.

A gate arch—Beaver Creek and Trail Gulch Trails

From the junction of Power Line Trail and Trail Gulch Trail, turn right. It is an easy 1.7 miles back to the junction with the Beaver Creek Trail, then another 0.8 mile to the parking area and trailhead.

TRAIL GULCH TRAIL

General description: An under-utilized trail that offers fishing in East Beaver Creek, peace and quiet, rocky cliffs, and a few good campsites.

Elevation gain to 8,500' saddle: 2,400'

Elevations: Highest: 8,500'   Lowest: 6,100'

Miles (round trip to 8,500' saddle): 11

Rating: Moderate to difficult

USGS topo maps: Mount Big Chief, Mount Pittsburg, Phantom Canyon

Users: Horses, backpackers, hikers

Trail Gulch Trail follows the Beaver Creek Trail for the first 0.8 mile (see "Beaver Creek Trail" description). Once it leaves the Beaver Creek drainage, it follows an intermittent creek (crossing often) for 1.7 miles to the junction with the Power Line (Pole) Trail that can be taken over the ridge back to the Beaver Creek drainage. This section of Trail Gulch Trail is easy, gaining just 500'. In contrast, in the next 3.0 miles beyond the Power Line Trail junction, the trail climbs 1,800', sometimes very steeply, to an 8,500' saddle. Some of the trail is rocky. The trail continues to cross the intermittent creek often until 0.5 mile below the saddle.

From the 8,500' saddle, the trail in the next mile loses 500' elevation and regains 200' elevation as it goes over a smaller saddle (8,200'), just before reaching the East Beaver Creek drainage. On the north side of the 8,200' saddle, the trail disappears in a meadow. Cross through the meadow toward East Beaver Creek, where the trail begins again next to the creek. The meadow is a lovely campsite, but it may be shared with cattle.

The trail continues north with many crossings of East Beaver Creek. It becomes private property, so don't plan to follow the trail and road along East Beaver Creek to Gold Camp Road. The road south along East Beaver Creek from Gold Camp Road is washed out at Mile 1.3, and in less than another mile, a huge locked steel gate and "No Trespassing" sign should discourage you from any thoughts of a one-way trip.

TABLE MOUNTAIN TRAIL

General description: A combination of trails and roads on State Trust Land and in the Beaver Creek State Wildlife Area.

Elevation gain: 900'

Elevations: Highest: 6,800'
Lowest (parking at 8-mile marker): 5,900'

Miles (in area described): 6.25

Rating: Easy

USGS topo maps: Mount Pittsburg, Phantom Canyon

Users: Hikers, hunters

Road directions: Follow the road directions for Beaver Creek and Trail Gulch Trails except that at the 8-mile marker on Fremont County Road 132, turn right (east) onto a primitive road and drive 0.2 mile to the parking area.

Table Mountain Trail is not an official name for the trails and roads in this area, but since the network is on Table Mountain and surrounding area, the name seems appropriate. The routes on State Trust Land have special use restrictions. It is very important to note that the State Trust Land is closed from June 1 through August 31. Camping and horseback riding are prohibited except during big game season.

If two cars are available, a nice 4.4-mile shuttle can be done. Beginning from the mile marker 8 parking area, you must first negotiate a crossing of Beaver Creek. In high water and when the water is too cold for wading, this could be an obstacle to hiking this trail. Cross the creek near the old homestead and hike north (upstream), going through the fence line and continuing through the meadow. Near the top of the meadow, the trail forks. The fork to the left returns to Beaver Creek and can be explored if you retrace your steps. Just beyond this junction on the right fork, the trail crosses a ditch and enters the trees, going through a second fence line about 50 yards beyond the ditch crossing. The trail continues to gain elevation as it delightfully meanders through the trees and crosses meadows. The trail is steep and rocky in places. After 2.0 miles the trail reaches a road. This 2-mile section is on state wildlife land. Once at the road, hiking 0.25 mile in either direction puts you on State Trust Land.

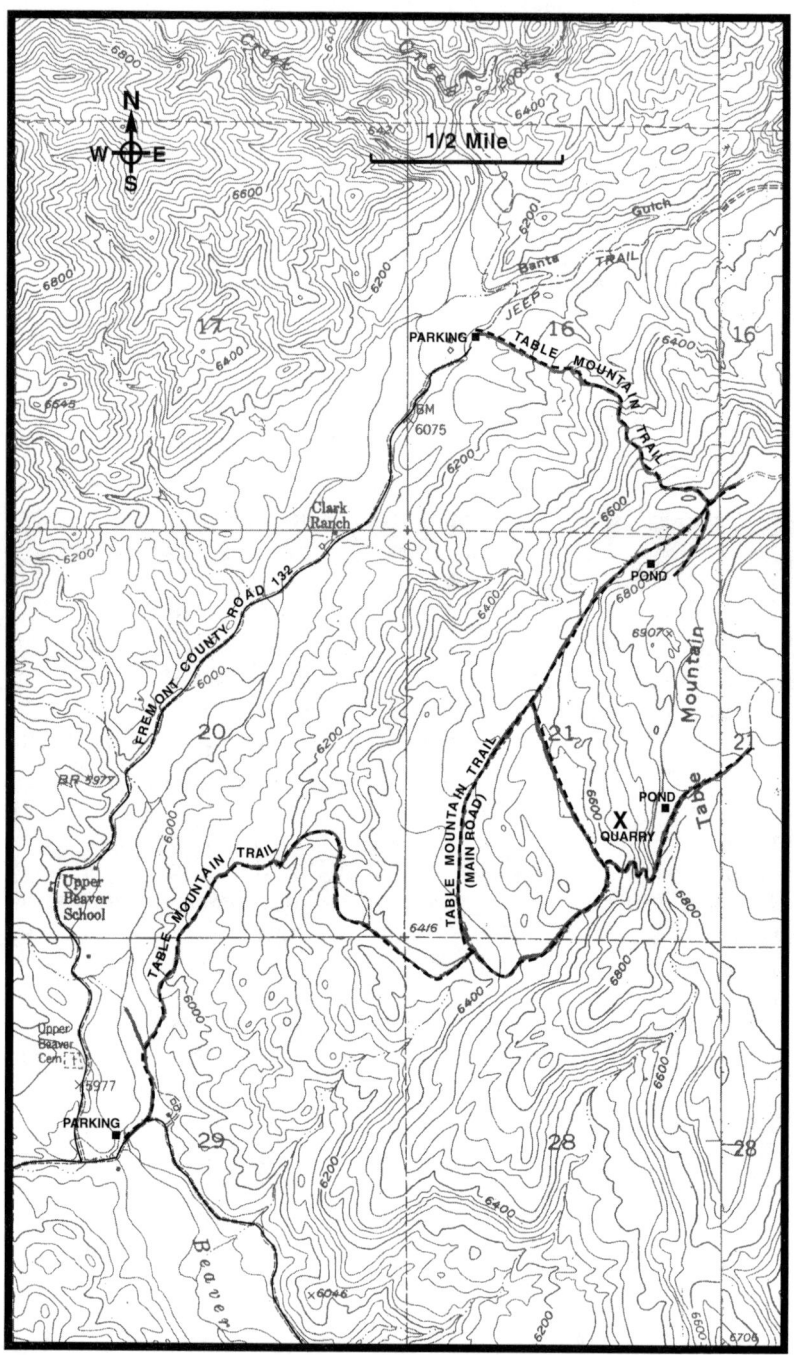

There are no signs to tell you when the State Trust Land begins, so in the summer months, it is probably best to turn around when you reach the road.

From this road junction, the shortest shuttle route is to the left (northwest). An alternate, but longer, route is to the right and is discussed below. For now take the shortest route and continue on the road to the left. After 0.7 mile from the trail and road junction, watch for a more primitive road coming in from the right (east). This is the north end of the alternate route. In another 0.5 mile watch for a pond, which may be dry, on the right side of the road. Look at the hillside above the pond to find a road cut through the vegetation. As you continue hiking northeast from the pond 0.2 mile, follow this cut down the hillside with your eyes. When it disappears into a grassy area at the base of the hill, you should be within a few feet of the junction for the route down to the parking area at the end of FC 132. The route down is on the left side of the road and is marked by cairns, but it is very easy to miss, and the road continues on farther than you probably care to hike. If you reach a quarry, you have missed the junction by almost a mile. You'll need to retrace your steps.

The 1.0-mile trail down to the parking area from the road goes over a small ridge before beginning its descent. Mostly the trail is the remnants of an old road, sometimes steep and rocky, that switchbacks down the ridge. Once at the parking area, you will need to climb over a barbed wire fence, fortunately made easier by some wood crossbeams at the corner of the parking lot. If you start the hike from this end, note that the trail is behind the State Trust Land sign and the power pole on the southeast side of the parking area. From the parking lot, the trail looks more like a dry wash than a trail. The parking area is in the Beaver Creek State Wildlife Area, but once you cross the fence you are quickly on State Trust Land.

For a 4.8-mile shuttle, take the alternate route by turning right (southeast) instead of left after the 2.0-mile section from the mile marker 8 parking area. In 0.1 mile the road turns northeast. It continues mostly northeast for the next 0.5 mile, where it breaks out into a small open area at the base of a quarry. There are several quarries in the area. This one has a backdrop cliff with a wide band of red rock. A faint side road heading southeast from here leads via switchbacks to the top of a plateau. Once at the top of the plateau, the road continues northeast to a pond (probably dry) and meadow in about 0.2 mile. Cross the dam of the pond or skirt the pond on the northern edge, heading westerly through the meadow to the plateau edge. It's a great view of the countryside and quarry below and a nice place for lunch. This side trip will add 1.5 miles and 200' elevation gain to your shuttle hike. There are several roads on top of this broad plateau, which can be explored. Keep track of where you are.

Retrace your steps to the base of the quarry and continue north. Shortly, the trail splits into two faint trails. Either trail works since they come together in a meadow after a very short descent. Continue your hike northwest until it reaches the main road. From the junction at the base of the quarry, going north, the main road is 0.5 mile. To continue the shuttle, turn right (northeast) on the main road and head up the hill.

All the trails described here are on the Phantom Canyon topo map but it is very helpful to have the Mount Pittsburg map.

HOLBERT TRAIL

General description: A canyon walk with structures from another day and with access to the Beaver Creek Wilderness Study Area.

Elevation gain: 1,200'

Elevations: Highest (at saddle above West Mill Creek): 8,300'
Lowest: 7,100'

Miles (round trip to saddle, without side trip): 7.5

Rating: Moderate

USGS topo map: Phantom Canyon

Users: Hikers

Road directions: From the junction of US 50 and CO 67 at the traffic light (4.2 miles west of Penrose on US 50), drive 13.7 miles north on CO 67 (Phantom Canyon Road) to the Steel Bridge. The pavement ends in 5.0 miles from US 50 and the road becomes narrow and winding, so drive with caution. You'll pass through two tunnels before reaching the Steel Bridge. Enjoy the slow drive as the canyon is gorgeous.

The Steel Bridge is an Historic Landmark. At one time a Bureau of Land Management information sign at the Steel Bridge said:

STEEL BRIDGE

Phantom Canyon 1899. Three passenger trains are running daily along the narrow gauge rails of the Florence and Cripple Creek. Among those aboard are prospectors eager to find their fortunes in the high mountain gold camps of Cripple Creek and Victor. Twelve stations keep track of the numerous freight trains carrying coal, produce, and supplies up to the mining camps, and gold ore down to the reduction mills in Florence.

Between 1894 and 1912, over 150 million dollars worth of gold ore was transported through Phantom Canyon on the Florence and Cripple Creek Railroad. This is the only original bridge remaining along the line. When the railroad was dismantled in 1915, three locomotives were attached by cable to one of the piers in an attempt to remove the trestle, but it would not budge. The bridge is now listed on the National Register of Historic Places.

The Steel Bridge, looking north—Holbert trailhead

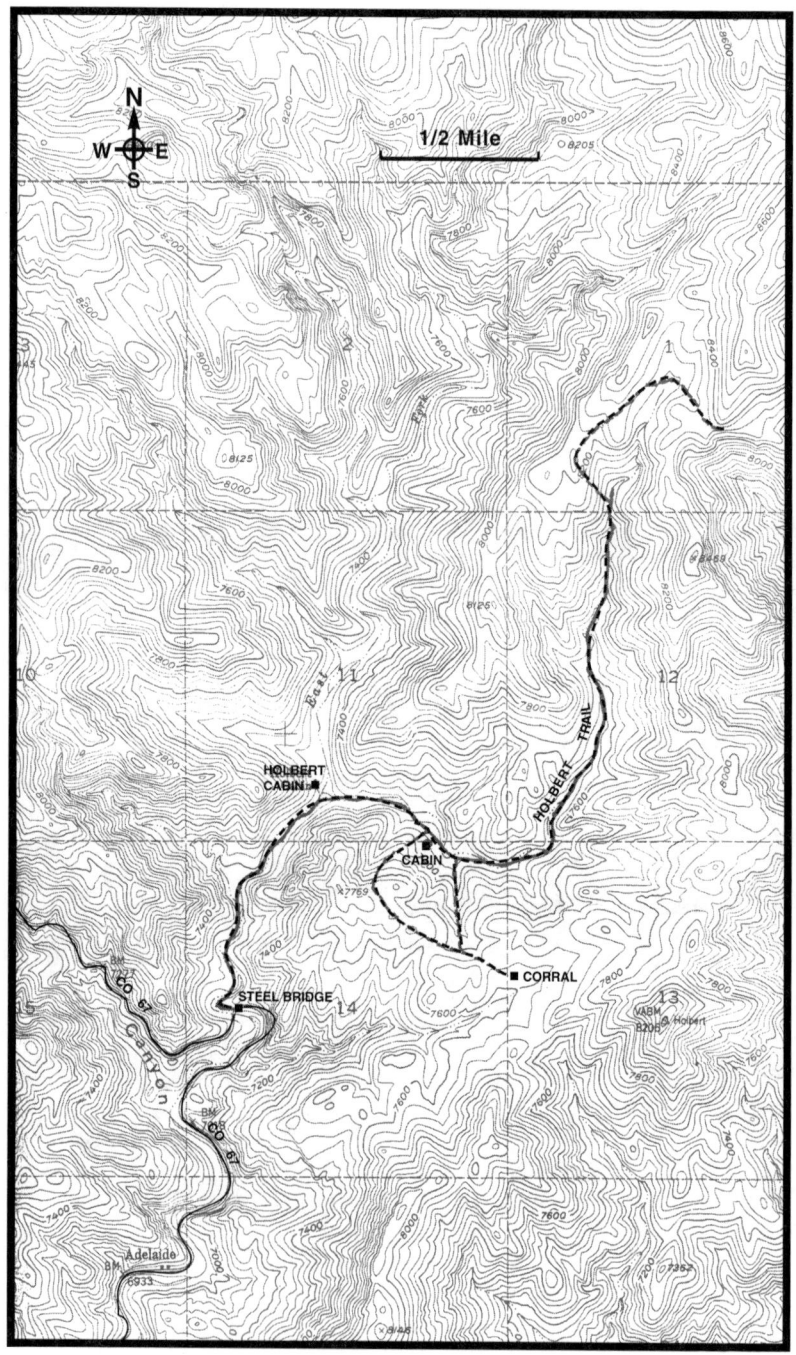

The current historical signs, just before the Steel Bridge to the left of the road, are worth reading.

The gate on the right side of the road at the Steel Bridge (don't cross the bridge) is the beginning of the Holbert Trail. You can park here in the area provided, or go through the gate (close it behind you) and drive a semi-rough 0.2 mile to the first stream crossing to park. A locked gate just across the creek prevents driving farther up this road.

Much of the **Holbert Trail** is on private property with several structures from earlier days. Please stay on the trail and do not vandalize the private property, as vandalism will certainly result in a trail closure. It's pretty country, with the upper section of the trail in the Beaver Creek Wilderness Study Area. Cattle may be grazing along the trail.

Assuming you've driven through the gate to the creek to park, begin the hike by making the first creek crossing and continuing up the road to the locked gate, which has walk-through access. The Holbert Cabin is 0.8 mile with seven more stream crossings. Stream crossings are generally not a problem. At the cabin go east (right), following a road. In 0.5 mile another cabin will be to the south at the Wilderness Boundary sign.

About 0.2 mile beyond the second cabin, a gully heads off to the south. This area can be tricky, so use your compass to continue east. The gully heading south has a trail and is worth exploring on the return trip. The side trail is steep in places with many windfallen trees across it, but it leads to an interesting brick structure. Once at the brick structure, you can hike east up an old road, over a saddle, and into a meadow. On the east side of the meadow is an old corral. A few yards west of the brick structure are the remains of two brick fireplaces. If you continue northwest along the road, it will turn northeast and descend to the Holbert Trail at the Wilderness Boundary sign on the west side of the second cabin.

But for now, continue east from this gully on the Holbert Trail for 0.3 mile, where the trail turns north. At this point, a draw to the northeast may tempt you, but be sure to hike into the left canyon, which heads north. The trail becomes sketchy once it turns north, but staying in the canyon bottom works well. At 2.75 miles from the trailhead, the upper end of the canyon has so much blow-down that hiking becomes frustrating. You may wish to climb out of the canyon on the west side (to the left), bushwhack north for 0.5 mile up the creek, then cross the creek to the east side and gain the saddle above West Mill Creek for a nice view down to the Beaver Creek drainage.

Holbert Cabin—Holbert Trail

PUEBLO AREA

PUEBLO TRAILS

Overview: Pueblo is fortunate to have a 35.0-mile asphalt/concrete trail system within the city limits and west to Pueblo Reservoir. The trail system offers benches, picnic tables and shelters, fishing docks, restrooms, drinking water, and wheelchair access. Hikers, bikers, joggers, rollerbladers, and horse riders make use of various sections of the trail system. Expect some trail sections and some picnic areas to be in need of repair. Improvements are made as time and money allow. The Pueblo Trails are broken into eight subsections. The descriptions begin at the northeast end, go south, and then west.

Elevation: 4,700'

Rating: Easy

Map: www.coloradolottery.com/about/trailmaps

UNIVERSITY PARK TRAIL

Miles (one way): 1.25

Users: Bikers, hikers

The **University Park Trail** access is at Bluestem Boulevard near Silverweed Court. There is only limited parking available at this access. The trail partly follows a drainage in its distance to Fountain Creek. Restrooms are available at the nearby shopping mall on Fountain Creek.

PUEBLO MALL TRAIL

Miles (one way): 1.0

Users: Bikers, hikers

From the north side of the CO 47 bridge over Fountain Creek, the trail crosses the bridge, then loops down under the bridge before climbing away from Fountain Creek to the intersection of University Boulevard and Dillon Drive. At the intersection the trail turns south and skirts around a pond, then continues behind a couple of businesses before ending at 29th Street. Facilities are available at the Pueblo Mall.

FOUNTAIN CREEK TRAIL

Miles (one way): 4

Users: Bikers, hikers

The **Fountain Creek Trail** runs south from CO 47 at Fountain Creek to the Fountain Creek Bridge crossing. There is access on the north end of the trail at Montebello Road and Haaff Elementary School. Access from 11th Street offers a picnic area with shelters (no restrooms). The El Centro De Quinto Sol Park (Trailhead Park) access on Erie Avenue between 8th and 4th Streets offers picnic shelters, drinking water, restrooms, and parking. South of 4th Street, Plaza Verde Park has tennis and basketball courts, playground equipment, parking, picnic shelters, drinking water, and restrooms, with access to the trail over the railroad track. The south end access of Fountain Creek Trail is from Joplin Avenue and has parking and picnic shelters (no restrooms). Fountain and Runyon Lakes are 0.5 mile to the west.

RUNYON LAKE TRAIL

Miles (one way): 1.75

Users: Horses, bikers, hikers

Runyon Lake Trail runs from the Fountain Creek Bridge at the Joplin Avenue access on the east, south of Fountain Lake, and around Runyon Lake to Runyon Crossing Bridge over the Arkansas River on the west end. Access to Runyon Crossing Bridge is from Moffat Avenue off Santa Fe Drive. Access from the north is via Locust Street off Santa Fe Avenue. The Locust Street access to Runyon Lake has lakeside parking, restrooms, and wheelchair-accessible fishing docks. It also gives access to the Arkansas Riverwalk in downtown Pueblo (see "Arkansas Riverwalk—Pueblo" section). A restroom is available on the east end of Runyon Lake near Fountain Lake. There is a 1.25-mile loop around Runyon Lake.

ARKANSAS RIVERWALK—PUEBLO

Miles (loop): 1.2

Users: Hikers

The **Arkansas Riverwalk—Pueblo** follows a 0.6-mile section of the old riverbed. Dedicated on October 6, 2000, this is a real treasure for Pueblo. It's a delightful place anytime but features special events throughout the year at the gazebo. Weddings are held along the Riverwalk. You can rent a paddleboat or take a tour boat ride in season (nominal fee). You can catch a bite to eat or take a stroll through the Union Avenue District and sample its eateries or do some shopping.

On the southeast end of the Riverwalk is a 0.9-mile connecting trail to Runyon Lake. The trail goes over Fay's Crossing Bridge, which spans I-25. An historic marker on the west end of the bridge reads, in part, as follows:

> In 1905 the Pueblo Bridge Company constructed the Elson Bridge for Las Animas County, Colorado. The bridge, originally located across the Purgatoire River on County Road 36, four miles northeast of El Moro, was one of the oldest roadways across the river.
>
> Only 16 feet wide, the bridge was not designed for the size and weight of modern motor vehicles. Consequently in the early 1990s the Colorado Department of Transportation scheduled the bridge for destruction and replacement. It was then when former City Council President Fay B. Kastelic expressed interest in adopting the bridge through Colorado Department of Transportation's Adopt-a-Bridge Program.
>
> The bridge was disassembled, transported and reassembled on June 9, 1995.
>
> It is in honor and appreciation of the dedication, persistence and service of Fay B. Kastelic that this historic crossways be named "FAY'S CROSSING."

Once over the bridge, the trail follows Thomas Phelps Creek to Runyon Lake.

ARKANSAS RIVER TRAIL EAST

Miles (one way): 3.7

Users: Horses, bikers, hikers

The **Arkansas River Trail East** follows the Arkansas River along its south bank from the Runyon Crossing Bridge at Santa Fe Avenue on the east to the Burkhardt Bridge at City Park on the west. Access is available at Main Street (Mile 0.7 from Runyon Crossing Bridge). Access at the Union Avenue Bridge (Mile 0.9) is via 81 steps. Access is also available from the 4th Street Bridge at Lincoln Avenue (Mile 1.3), Dutch Clark Stadium (Mile 1.8), Wildhorse Creek Bridge (Mile 2.2), Reservoir Street (Mile 2.9), and City Park Ballfield 3 (Mile 3.7). A picnic area (no restrooms) with gazebo and fireplace grates is at Mile 3.2 from Runyon Bridge Crossing or 0.5 mile east of the Burkhardt Bridge. The Wildhorse Creek and Burkhardt Bridges give access to the Arkansas River Trail West on the north side of the Arkansas River. City Park offers several facilities including ballfields, tennis courts, zoo, duck ponds, swimming pool in season, picnic shelters, drinking water, and restrooms.

ARKANSAS RIVER TRAIL WEST

Miles (one way): 6.9

Users: Horses, bikers, hikers

The **Arkansas River Trail West**, on the north side of the Arkansas River, begins at the junction of 18th Street and Graham Avenue on the north at Wildhorse Creek Park and ends at Pueblo Reservoir Dam on the west.

At the Gardner Pump Station (Mile 0.5 from the junction of 18th Street and Graham Avenue) a road forks off to the left. Follow this road south to parking, a restroom, and the Wildhorse Creek Bridge, which gives access to the Arkansas River Trail East. Or you can continue on the Arkansas River Trail West another 0.25 mile (where it turns west), then follow a rough road and path 0.1 mile east along the river to these facilities.

At Mile 1.5 on the Arkansas River Trail West, the trail follows a road for 0.1 mile, crossing a railroad track. At Mile 2.2 from the 18th Street trailhead is a junction. The trail to the south (left) crosses the

Burkhardt Bridge, giving access to City Park and the Arkansas River Trail East. The Arkansas River Trail West continues west 1.2 miles to the Nature Center, which has parking, picnicking, a café, fishing dock, restrooms, bike rental, playground equipment, and interpretive programs.

Arkansas River from Greenway and Nature Center—Arkansas River Trail West

Two trails (one asphalt and one concrete) run west from the Nature Center with one crossover path before they rejoin as one in about 0.3 mile. The older asphalt section of the trail follows the river while the new concrete section follows the bluffs. If you use these two trails to make a loop trip, the shortest loop is 0.3 mile using the crossover path, while the longest loop is 0.7 mile. Poison ivy grows along both trails.

From the west end of the loop, the trail continues 1.2 miles on a concrete section to the east end of the Rock Canyon picnic areas. In 1995 the asphalt section that followed the river from this point was closed to allow gravel mining. Gravel mining ceased in 2003 and hopefully the pit will become a small lake, and additional restoration projects will create a riparian area once again.

The trail continues through the Rock Canyon picnic areas with fishing pond, swimming and water slide lake, and many picnic sites. At the water slide (3.0 miles from the Nature Center) a side trail to the south (left) crosses the Arkansas River on a foot bridge to access additional picnic facilities and parking. When the trail junctions 0.2 mile west of the water slide, the north (right) fork goes to the North Shore Marina, 5.0 miles distant. Along this route are camping and picnic facilities, with a junction at 3.9 miles leading to Pueblo West.

From the junction 0.2 mile west of the water slide, the west fork can be followed to the base of the dam in 0.25 mile. From the Nature Center it is 3.5 miles west to the Pueblo Reservoir Dam. Other choices at the dam include crossing the Arkansas River and following the trail 2.1 miles, either to CO 96 (left fork at the trail junction at the south end of the dam) or to the South Shore Marina (right fork at the junction). The South Shore Marina has a trail system that leads to the top of the bluff behind the Arkansas Point Campground (see "Pueblo Reservoir Trails—Arkansas Point Trails" section).

Lake Pueblo State Park requires a Colorado State Parks Pass for vehicle access to its facilities.

PUEBLO BOULEVARD—NORTHERN AVENUE TRAILS

Miles in subsection: 5.6

Users: Bikers, hikers

From the Arkansas River Trail East at Burkhardt Bridge, a trail meanders through City Park to Goodnight Avenue (0.4 mile), then follows the east side of Pueblo Boulevard south 2.4 miles to Northern Avenue. The trail continues east on the north side of Northern Avenue for 1.0 mile to Cambridge Avenue/Moore Avenue. On the south side of Northern Avenue the trail runs 1.8 miles from Wedgewood Drive on the east end to Encino Drive on the west end.

PUEBLO RESERVOIR TRAILS

General description: Trails, old roads, ravines, and open prairie offer a variety of outings in the Pueblo Reservoir State Wildlife Area and at Lake Pueblo State Park.

Rating: Easy

Users: Horses, mountain bikers, hikers

Overview: The west end of Pueblo Reservoir is a State Wildlife Area and does not require an entrance fee. The east end of the Reservoir, near the dam, is Lake Pueblo State Park. Because it is a Colorado State Park, an entrance fee is required for vehicle access.

Besides the paved trail from the Rock Canyon picnic areas to the North Shore Marina (see "Pueblo Trails—Arkansas River Trail West" section), Pueblo Reservoir has several dirt trails on the south side. A series of trails run between the South Shore Marina and CO 96 (see "Arkansas Point Trails" section). The Conduit Nature Trail is located at the Swallows on the west end of the Reservoir. Between the Arkansas Point Trails access on CO 96 and the Conduit Nature Trail accesses are 18 additional access points to Pueblo Reservoir and Division of Wildlife lands that offer a road, a trail, a ravine, or just the prairie as your guide. When picking your access point, watch for private property signs. Please stay off private property in this area. There is enough state land to explore without harassing private landowners.

Park only in designated areas. Camping and campfires are not allowed. Fishing and seasonal hunting are available. Wear shoes that will protect your ankles and feet from cactus thorns. Take plenty of water, especially on a hot day. Because these prairies are so arid it is a very fragile environment. Please respect it.

Some of the wildlife that may be encountered include deer, coyotes, prairie dogs, beavers, cottontails, jackrabbits, lizards, snakes, and birds, including eagles and great blue herons.

When cabin fever strikes during those short winter days, these trails are an excellent choice to explore during Pueblo's mild winters. The cooler temperatures of winter are even preferred over the hot summer days.

For more information, contact Division of Parks and Outdoor Recreation, 640 Pueblo Reservoir Road, Pueblo, CO 81005, (719) 561-9320.

ARKANSAS POINT TRAILS

Elevations: Highest: 5,148'   Lowest: 4,950'

USGS topo maps: Northwest Pueblo, Southwest Pueblo

Road directions: The Arkansas Point Trails system can be reached either from the South Shore Marina, if you have a Colorado State Parks Pass, or from a limited parking area on CO 96. The main entrance road to the South Shore Marina at Pueblo Reservoir is from CO 96, 4.0 miles west of the Pueblo Boulevard and Thatcher Avenue intersection. If you have a Parks Pass, you can follow the entrance road to the South Shore Marina and park your vehicle near the ranger station at the Arkansas Point Campground or in the parking areas used by the boaters. If you plan to park on CO 96, drive another 0.8 mile west of the main reservoir entrance. If you reach Red Creek Springs Road East, you are 0.2 mile west of the CO 96 parking area.

The area of the **Arkansas Point Trails** system encompasses about one square mile. The trails are not marked on the topographic maps except for the road leading from CO 96 to the bluff overlooking the Arkansas Point Campground. But with Bogg's Creek and the Wet Mountains to the west, CO 96 to the south and southeast, the Pueblo Reservoir access road to the east, and the South Shore Marina, the Reservoir, and Pikes Peak to the north, you won't get lost. A section of the Arkansas Valley Conduit can be seen below the bluff near the Arkansas Point Campground and is identified on the map, so it can be used as an additional reference point. Bogg's Creek may be a creek or a lake, depending on the rise and fall of Pueblo Reservoir.

This limited description of the trail system is from the South Shore Marina access point. A trail begins on the west side of the ranger station and heads east toward the campground. A trail junction allows a loop trip that will take you to the top of the bluff, where the views are outstanding. Follow the trail counter-clockwise to the top of the bluff, to an old road and junction. The road to the right at this junction becomes a trail that dead-ends on the west end of the bluff. The trail at the far end of this bluff is not for those with acrophobia.

To continue the loop hike, turn left from the junction and follow the road east on the top of the bluff for 0.2 mile, where the road will turn south. Here a trail to the left (north) drops back to the campground to complete the loop. The loop trip is less than a mile.

Before you return to the campground, you may wish to follow the road south for 0.8 mile to the CO 96 parking area. Along this road, several trails and side roads head west. These trails and side roads lead out to the ends of several bluffs overlooking Bogg's Creek or go down the gullies to Bogg's Creek. From Bogg's Creek a trail leads north, back to the South Shore Marina. This allows many variations for hiking, mountain biking, or horse riding. Benches have been placed at several places along these trails. Take a moment to enjoy the views or watch the hawks fly overhead.

CONDUIT NATURE TRAIL

Elevation gain: 120'

Elevations: Highest: 5,060' Lowest: 4,940'

Miles (loop to end of trail): 1.5

USGS topo map: Swallows

Road directions: The Conduit Nature Trail with its three access trails is located at the west end of Pueblo Reservoir. To reach the trailheads, take CO 96 10.6 miles west from the intersection of Pueblo Boulevard and Thatcher Avenue to the Lake Pueblo State Park access road. Follow the access road 0.6 mile to a junction. Turn north (left) onto the gravel road into the State Wildlife Area, and follow this road for 5.0 miles to the first access point. A second access point is at Mile 5.2, and the third access point is down the hill at Mile 5.8.

The **Conduit Nature Trail** was constructed in 1974 by the Pueblo Conservation Corps, a group of high school students from all over Colorado. The Arkansas Valley Conduit was constructed in 1907 to bring water from the river to the CF&I Steel Mill (now Rocky Mountain Steel Mills) in Pueblo. The ditch last carried water in 1946.

As you hike this trail, contemplate the engineering feat of the conduit. Note the outcroppings of sandstone, limestone, and shale that once were the bottom of a large, shallow, interior ocean before uplifting, folding, faulting, and subsequent erosion gave this area its present appearance. The trail along the ridge gives some nice views of Pikes Peak and the Arkansas River Valley. Please stay on the trails to help preserve this historic area.

Except for a couple of dips through small gullies, the first access point steadily descends to the Conduit Nature Trail. As this access trail nears the Conduit Nature Trail, it parallels a gully to the east. The remains of an old foundation are found along the trail, just above the junction with the main trail. Looking east across the gully, there is a nice view from this old foundation to the Arkansas River Valley and to a section of both the Conduit Nature Trail and the conduit itself.

The second access point has one drop through a small gully before reaching the top of a ridge, and then descends slightly to the main Conduit Nature Trail. This access trail joins the main Conduit Nature Trail just east of where the third access trail reaches the ridge top.

The third access, at the bottom of the bluff, has a restroom, ample parking, and both ends of a loop trail. If the trail is followed counter-clockwise, it zigzags its way up the cliff via four switchbacks to the conduit. Once at the conduit, an interesting side trip can be made by hiking west on the north side to a bridge that crosses the conduit. This side trail ends at the top of one of the U-shaped siphon tubes designed to carry water from one bluff to another. The other end of the siphon tube can be seen across the valley to the west. Retrace your steps to continue east along the Conduit Nature Trail.

Continuing east, the Conduit Nature Trail crosses the conduit to the south side, going almost to the top of the ridge, and reaches the second access trail. It eventually drops into the conduit and crosses it at various points. The first access trail joins the main trail just before the trail begins to descend to the valley floor.

At the bottom of the valley is a trail junction. The trail to the left (west) returns to the main parking area to complete the loop. The trail to the east (right) enters the bottom of a large gully. Watch for the continuation of the trail as an obscure path that leads up the other side of the gully. Once out of the gully the trail is good to its end, just a short distance to the east. A more obvious side trail stays in the gully and leads to a closer look at a second U-shaped siphon tube. There is a wonderful picnic site and fire ring on the south side of the siphon tube, but remember **fires are prohibited**.

MISCELLANEOUS TRAILS

USGS topo maps: Hobson, Swallows

From the Conduit Nature Trail access at the base of the bluff, the road continues west another 3.5 miles, then ends for low-clearance vehicles at a river fishing access loop. Along this 3.5 miles are six walk-in access points to the river. These access points are overgrown with weeds but do offer alternatives for short hiking trips.

Miles (round trip): 2

USGS topo map: Northwest Pueblo

On the south side of the Arkansas River east of the Pueblo Reservoir Dam is a parking area used mostly by fishermen. This parking area is 2.4 miles west on CO 96 from the intersection of Pueblo Boulevard and Thatcher Avenue. A network of roads leaves the west end of the parking lot and eventually leads to the east end of the Pueblo Fish Hatchery. From the east end of the fish hatchery, a trail and the river bed can be followed to the Rock Canyon picnic area on the south side of the Arkansas River. The rustic trail is only 1.0 mile long, but once at the picnic area, there is access to the river trails on the north side of the river.

RYE AREA

APACHE FALLS TRAIL #1311

General description: Features a spectacular waterfall, if high creek crossings, downed timber, and an overgrown trail don't discourage you.

Elevation gain: 1,360'

Elevations: Highest: 8,600'   Lowest: 7,240'

Miles (round trip): 6

Rating: Moderate

USGS topo map: Hayden Butte

Users: Hikers

Road directions: The shortest route to Apache Falls is southwest of Rye through private property off the Lascar Road. **However, public abuse of the private property has essentially closed off this access to the public. It is highly recommended that you use the Bartlett Trail approach.** If you do decide to attempt Apache Falls from the Lascar Road, you **MUST** obtain permission from the landowner to cross the private property. If you are declined permission, please respect the landowner's wishes.

    To contact the landowner and reach the trailhead, take Lascar Road (Exit 64) off I-25. The road heads west for 5.2 miles before making a jog north for 0.25 mile, then heads west again for another mile, and finally turns north to follow along the base of the mountains. Watch for mile marker 8. The road crosses South Apache Creek 0.3 mile north of mile marker 8. If the creek is high, plan to hike elsewhere, as the ten or eleven South Apache Creek crossings are difficult to negotiate in high water. Take the right fork at the South Apache Creek crossing to contact the landowner. If you have obtained permission, the faint trailhead is 0.2 mile north of the South Apache Creek crossing, and the end of the road is 0.1 mile farther.

    The road ends at a farmhouse with turnaround space outside the gate. If you missed seeing the faint trailhead, backtrack the 0.1 mile and park along the road just south of the private metal gate that is on the west side of the road. A fenced meadow on the east side of the road has a power line running east and west on its north edge. There's a large pine tree on the south edge of the meadow.

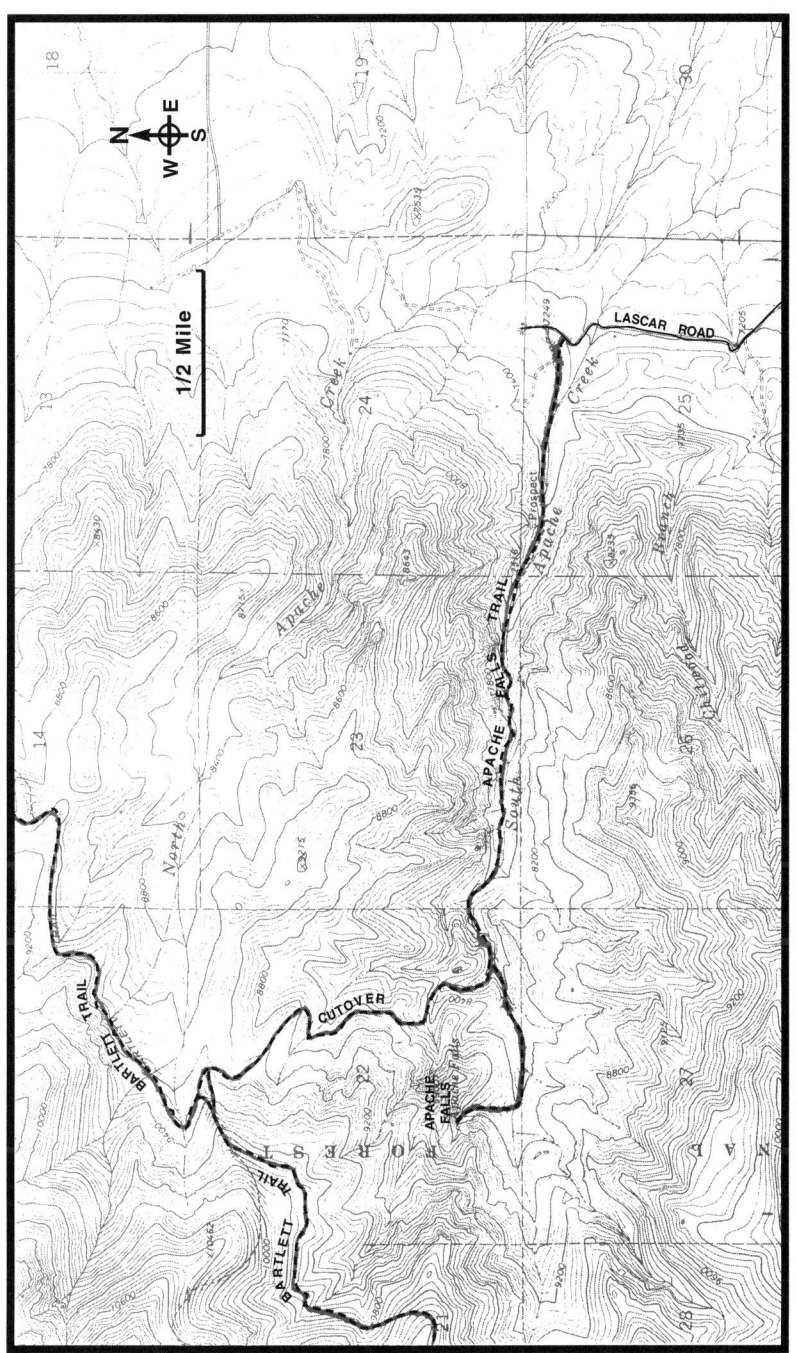

Apache Falls, not visible until you're at its base, drops 100' into a pool during the summer. If you're lucky enough to be here in the winter, the falls are sometimes a 100' column of ice, sculpted with stalactites and stalagmites. In the stillness of a winter day, water trickles behind the ice column and ice chunks may crash to the base. Apache Falls is as spectacular in the winter as it is refreshing in the summer.

Because Apache Falls cannot be seen until you're at its base, finding it can sometimes be difficult. The creek crossings make the 3.0-mile trail seem longer. The trail is in the trees, so judging your location on the map using side canyons or other natural features can be impossible. If trail conditions are good it can take two hours to reach the falls. If you're fighting downed timber, overgrown vegetation in the summer, an icy trail in the winter, or high creek crossings in the spring, it can take much longer. It's not fun counting creek crossings, but that gives you the best idea about the distance to the falls.

The **Apache Falls Trail** begins through the scrub oak on the west side of the road. This short trail quickly joins the road that is blocked by that metal gate (please don't climb over the gate). As you head west, the road forks. Take the left fork, which will take you slightly downhill to a closed gate at the edge of a meadow. Remember to re-close the gate after you go through. Hike through the meadow, staying on the north side of the creek, to the San Isabel National Forest Boundary 0.75 mile from the trailhead. **Please** stay on the trail as it crosses this private property. The forest boundary is marked by another gate. Please close it behind you.

The Apache Falls Trail can sometimes be overgrown with vegetation and periodically gets a lot of blow-down. Allow extra hiking time if trail searching and clambering over fallen timber is necessary.

Once you're on the National Forest property, the trail begins the creek crossings. The trail crosses the creek four times before reaching an icefall, visible in the winter, on the north facing canyon wall. This icefall marks the halfway point to Apache Falls. If the water in the creek is high, crossing #7 puts the trail between two major branches of the creek. So it'll take at least another crossing (count as #7b) to be completely on the south side of the creek.

After the next crossing (#8), which puts the trail on the north side of the creek, watch for a trail junction to the right. It is marked by a tall stump surrounded by rocks at its base. The trail to the right (north) is a cutover to the Bartlett Trail out of Rye. This cutover trail was the original Bartlett Trail. It has some downed timber and is becoming faint in places from disuse, but can be followed if the hiker stays alert. When South Apache Creek is high, this trail can be used to reach Apache Falls, avoiding most of the creek crossings as well as the private property. This access to the falls is almost twice as long and there is a 1,200' elevation loss dropping down to South Apache Creek from the Bartlett Trail. But seeing the additional water in Apache Falls in the spring makes it worth the effort. The cutover trail gives some nice vistas (see "Bartlett Trail" section).

A trail marker—junction of Apache Falls Trail and cutover trail to Bartlett Trail

Taking the left fork from this junction, the trail continues along South Apache Creek, crossing it two more times. At the second crossing (#10 from Lascar Road) the trail turns north toward Apache Falls. Halfway between South Apache Creek and Apache Falls, the trail crosses the creek that forms Apache Falls.

Once you've explored the base of the falls, you may wish to see it from a higher vantage point. If you have some experience with rock climbing, nerves of steel, or both, backtrack a few feet down the trail from the falls to the steep slope at the edge of the rocks on the northeast side of the creek. By scrambling up the slope next to the rocks, then carefully working your way across the rocks, you can get a beautiful view of the upper part of the falls. **Be careful!**

Apache Falls in June—Apache Falls Trail

BARTLETT TRAIL #1310

General description: Features access to Apache Falls, a climb of Greenhorn Mountain, a one-way trip with car shuttle, and some great views.

Option #1: *Elevation gain from trailhead to Apache Falls:* 1,800'

Elevation gain (return trip): 1,200'

Elevations: Highest: 9,400' Lowest: 8,000'

Miles (round trip): 11.2

Rating: Difficult

USGS topo maps: Hayden Butte, Rye

Users: Horses, hikers

Option #2: *Elevation gain from trailhead to Greenhorn Mountain:* 4,347'

Elevations: Highest: 12,347' Lowest: 8,000'

Miles (round trip): 16

Rating: Difficult

USGS topo maps: Badito Cone, Hayden Butte, Rye, San Isabel

Users: Hikers

Option #3: *Elevation gain from trailhead to waiting driver at end of Greenhorn Mountain Road:* 3,760'

Elevations: Highest: 11,760' Lowest: 8,000'

Miles (one way): 9.75

Rating: Difficult

USGS topo maps: Badito Cone, Hayden Butte, Rye, San Isabel

Users: Horses, hikers

Road directions: The Bartlett Trail is south of Rye. From the intersection of Main Street and Boulder Avenue in Rye, travel 0.9 mile south on Boulder Avenue to a "T" in the road at Granger Drive and

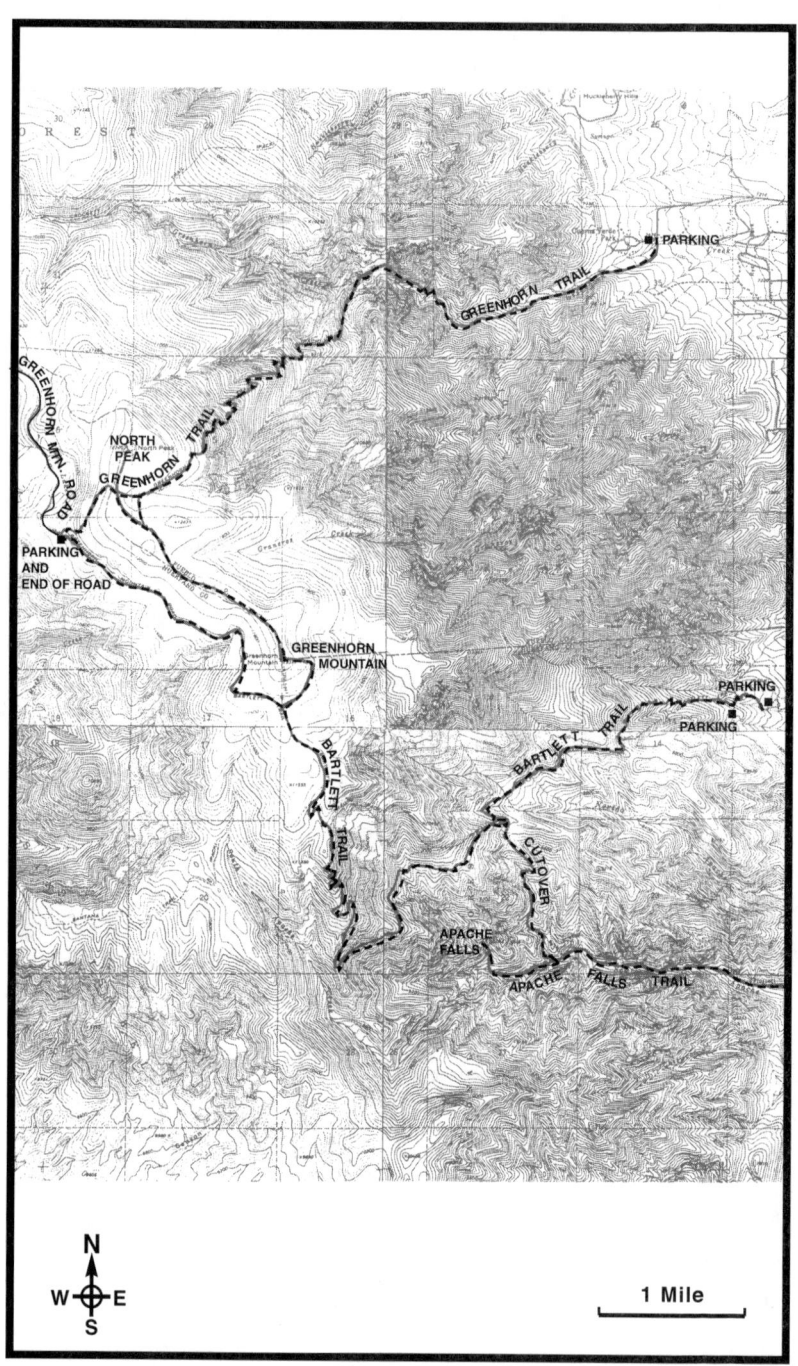

Hayes Lane. Drive east (left) on Granger for 0.2 mile, then turn south (right) onto Hunter Road. Follow Hunter Road 0.7 mile to Baxter Road. Turn west (right) onto Baxter Road and follow it 0.5 mile, then turn south (left). Follow the Bartlett Trail road 2.6 miles to limited parking for cars. Please respect the private residence here. The road just prior to this limited parking area can be very muddy when wet. From the limited parking area, high-clearance vehicles can follow the road another 0.3 mile to a larger parking area and the trailhead.

The **Bartlett Trail** is in the Greenhorn Mountain Wilderness Area, so mountain bikers and motorized vehicles are prohibited. The trail heads west from the upper parking area to a registration box and a junction (about two minutes up the trail). The left fork is the old Bartlett Trail as shown on topographic maps. It can be followed but, since it is not maintained, plan to climb over plenty of downed timber.

To follow the maintained trail take the right fork, which has several sets of switchbacks and some good views. At Mile 1.75 on a ridge top you may see the old Bartlett Trail coming in from the left (now blocked by logs across the trail). At Mile 2.75, the trail crosses North Apache Creek. North Apache Creek is not labeled but it is a sizable creek and is a good landmark if you plan to hike to Apache Falls via the cutover trail. Don't confuse the smaller intermittent creeks with North Apache Creek.

If you are hiking to Apache Falls from the Bartlett Trail, watch for a ridge heading east off the Bartlett Trail, about 0.3 mile (a ten-minute hike) after crossing North Apache Creek. Watch for a huge cairn on the right. The somewhat obscure cutover trail to Apache Falls goes out onto this ridge a few yards before beginning a short, but very steep, section as the trail descends toward South Apache Creek. This steep descent can be avoided by continuing along the Bartlett Trail beyond this ridge another 0.1 mile (one- to two-minute hike) to a trail that has a more gradual, but slightly longer descent. These two parts of the cutover trail join just below the steep section. The trail drops 1,200' to South Apache Creek in 1.75 miles. From the junction on South Apache Creek, there are two South Apache Creek crossings in the remaining 0.75 mile to Apache Falls. This route doesn't eliminate all creek crossings, but the number of difficult ones is more reasonable (see "Apache Falls Trail" section).

Continuing west from its junction with the cutover trail, the Bartlett Trail winds in and out of the gullies and ridges until it reaches the ridge south of Greenhorn Mountain. It then begins a series of switchbacks up the ridge until it reaches the broad plateau below and to the south of Greenhorn Mountain. At Mile 7.3, at the base of the mountain, is a trail junction.

If climbing Greenhorn Mountain is your destination, leave the trail at this junction and cut around the southeast flank of the mountain, gaining elevation as you go until you have gone beyond the scree, thereby reaching the Greenhorn summit from the east. Avoid climbing Greenhorn Mountain from the south side as it is all loose rock.

The Bartlett Trail continues to the west from the Mile 7.3 junction and reaches, at Mile 7.75, the end of the old Greenhorn Mountain Road, which is southwest of the top of Greenhorn Mountain. This section of the Greenhorn Mountain Road can no longer be driven in a vehicle. If you plan to have someone pick you up, you'll have another 2.0 miles to hike to reach the current end of Greenhorn Mountain Road. If your driver is fishing at the southernmost Blue Lake, add another 0.3 mile. This makes a fairly strenuous ten-mile hike.

GREENHORN TRAIL #1316

General description: Features climbs of Greenhorn Mountain or North Peak, a one-way hike with car shuttle, wildlife viewing, and nice views from above timberline.

Option #1: *Elevation gain from trailhead to Greenhorn Mountain:* 4,872'

Elevations: Highest: 12,347'   Lowest: 7,475'

Miles (one way): 9

Rating: Difficult

USGS topo maps: Rye, San Isabel

Users: Hikers

Option #2: *Elevation gain from trailhead to Greenhorn Mountain Road:* 4,565'

Elevations: Highest (at saddle): 12,040'   Lowest: 7,475'

Miles (one way): 8.5

Rating: Difficult

USGS topo maps: Rye, San Isabel

Users: Horses, backpackers, hikers

Road directions: The Greenhorn Trail is west of Rye. From the Main Street and Boulder Avenue intersection in Rye, go west on Main Street through town to the junction of Park Road and Cuerno Verde Road (0.6 mile). Either road will work. You can follow the Cuerno Verde Road (right fork) for 1.5 miles, where it makes a 90-degree turn to the south. Continue south 0.2 mile to a small parking area. If you've followed Park Road, the pavement ends in 0.7 mile at the Rye Mountain Park entrance. In another 0.1 mile the road forks. Take the right (north) fork, which in 0.4 mile intersects Cuerno Verde Road. Turn left (west) onto Cuerno Verde Road, which takes you to the 90-degree turn in 0.6 mile, and then to the parking area in another 0.2 mile. Respect the private property surrounding the parking area.

Greenhorn Trail descends the hill from the parking area to Greenhorn Creek and immediately crosses the creek on a bridge. The trail stays on the south side of the creek for the next 2.0 miles. This is a pleasant section of the trail, as it parallels Greenhorn Creek, but you'll hear the creek more than you'll see it. Also, a fence line runs between the trail and the creek for the first 0.5 mile, effectively keeping you from the creek. The trail will cross two small side creeks (at Mile 1.25 and Mile 1.7), and will split less than 0.2 mile after the second of these crossings. The fork to the right goes down to the creek to a very pleasant campsite. Just beyond this camping area on the main trail is the second crossing of Greenhorn Creek.

You'll encounter the "rock slide" at Mile 2.7. The third crossing of Greenhorn Creek is at Mile 3.0. Once across the creek, the trail disappears at a nice picnic and camping site. To pick up the trail again, hike downstream, noting the two large cairns along the route. Keep looking for the trail, which skirts beaver ponds off to the right. The side creek that feeds the beaver ponds is then crossed by the trail six times in less than 0.25 mile before the trail leaves the creek to begin the seemingly endless switchbacks that lead to timberline. Make sure you have plenty of water for this section.

From the trailhead it is 7.0 miles to timberline. If you're hiking to the top of Greenhorn Mountain, hike another 0.5 mile from timberline to the junction of two gullies. The small gully heads west-northwest while the much larger gully you're in turns southwest. The Greenhorn Trail at the junction of these two gullies ends as a defined path and is then marked by cairns to the saddle below North Peak. Leave the Greenhorn Trail at this point, hiking south along the larger gully. Either side of the gully works. Hike to the saddle between the 12,200' and 12,237' points. From this saddle, descend 160' to a saddle along the Greenhorn Mountain ridge. Skirt the next 12,200' point on the northeast side to another saddle. From this saddle note the location of a rocky shelter above the trees and along the ridge. Continue along the ridge (southeast) next to the trees. Once above the trees, head southeast toward the shelter (it won't be visible until your nearly there). From the shelter, turn south to follow the ridge for an easy 0.25-mile ascent to the top of Greenhorn Mountain. Watch for bighorn sheep and make use of their trails, when you can, on the northeast side of the Greenhorn Mountain ridge.

If you're not climbing Greenhorn Mountain but wish to continue the Greenhorn Trail to its end on Greenhorn Mountain Road, continue west from the junction of the two gullies. There are a few cairns to mark the trail, but hiking west to the low point south of North Peak works well. There is a cairn at the low point on the ridge south of North Peak. North Peak is an easy climb from the saddle, adding a 0.75-mile round trip to your hike. Greenhorn Mountain can also be climbed from the saddle by following the ridge for 2.0 miles, skirting the higher points along the ridge.

From the low point below North Peak, follow the cairns west until you pick up the well-defined trail, which descends in 0.75 mile to Greenhorn Mountain Road. The trail joins Greenhorn Mountain Road at the end of the driveable section.

Severe thunder and lightning storms can pass over the top of North Peak and Greenhorn Mountain. It's above timberline and very exposed, so keep an eye on the weather. Climbing Greenhorn Mountain from Rye is a strenuous hike requiring excellent physical condition. It's a great conditioning trail even if the summit is not reached.

MILLSET TRAIL #1317

General description: Reopened to the public in 1999, this trail climbs through meadows and forested areas, follows a section of Greenhorn Creek, passes an old cabin, and finally ends on Greenhorn Mountain Road.

Elevation gain (round trip): 3,400'

Elevations: Highest: 11,080' Lowest: 7,880'

Miles (one way): 6.5

Rating: Difficult

USGS topo maps: Rye, San Isabel

Users: Horses (to cabin only), hikers

Road directions: From the main turnoff to Rye, the Millset trailhead is 4.5 miles north on CO 165. Or watch for the San Isabel National Forest sign, which is 0.2 mile before the turnoff to the parking area. There is a Millset trailhead sign along CO 165, 0.1 mile before the parking area turnoff. If you are coming from San Isabel, drive 5.5 miles south on CO 165, or watch for the YMCA Camp Jackson entrance and proceed another 0.4 mile to the parking area turnoff.

The **Millset Trail** (formerly Camp Crockett Trail) leaves the parking area heading south through private property for the first 0.2 mile. Please stay on the trail. At Mile 0.6 the trail crosses a ridge and then begins a slight downhill for the next 0.25 mile, crossing under a power line, to a trail junction. The trail to the right goes to the YMCA Camp Jackson. In the next couple of miles the trail climbs steeply at times and for a while follows a section of old road, which stops at a small mine dig. There are three small meadows along this 2-mile section. When you get to a fourth meadow peppered with trees (Mile 3.0), watch for an old campfire ring (now converted to a cairn) beside the trail. You'll want to turn southwest (left) at this cairn and proceed up the hill through the meadow. The trail continues to climb, then levels off for a short distance in the vicinity of the 10,470' point. As you begin your 100' descent to Greenhorn Creek (about an 8-minute hike), you'll quickly pick up the sound of the creek. Once at the creek, watch for a rocky outcrop. The cabin is across the creek from this outcrop. It's a great place for lunch if you do not care to proceed farther. Please do not vandalize the cabin or any of the other

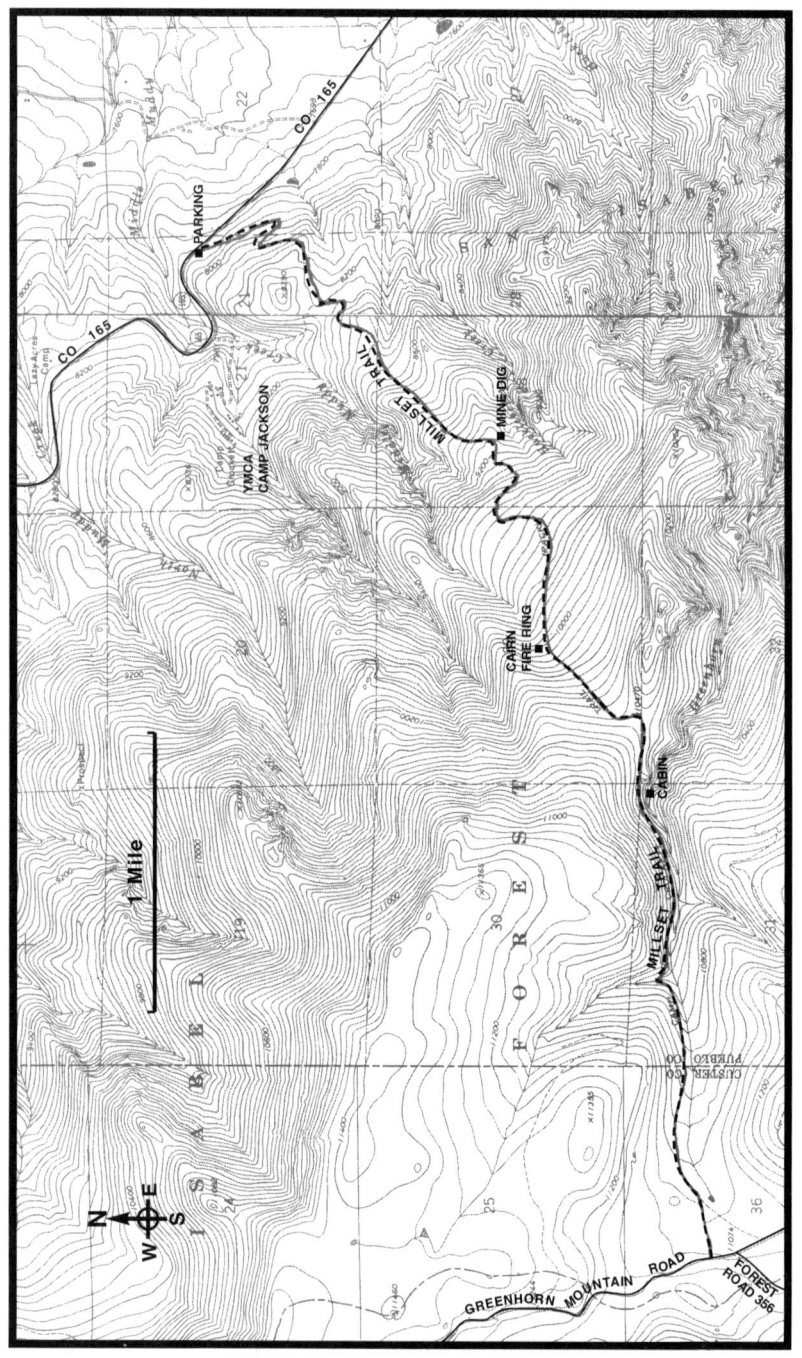

historic remains. The cabin is about 4.25 miles from the CO 165 trailhead.

If you continue on to Greenhorn Mountain Road from the cabin, the trail can get very sketchy at times, but a variety of trail markers (some very old) should keep you on track. The trail beyond the cabin follows Greenhorn Creek closely for a long mile. Once you've crossed a major side creek, the trail is more open. It eventually breaks out of the trees completely. From here it is 0.5 mile to the road without aid of a trail. Make note of where you exit the trees so that you can find the trail on your return trip. If you are headed for the road, hike west to the rocky outcrop. Once at the outcrop, Greenhorn Mountain Road is clearly visible. From the outcrop continue close to the trees for as long as possible until you need to leave the trees to make the shortest hike to the road. The meadow can be swampy, so look for grassy areas that are brown, indicative of drier ground. A cairn is built on a rock at the trailhead. Forest Road 356 (21 miles from CO 165 via Ophir Creek and Greenhorn Mountain Roads) is just south of the trailhead if you plan to have someone pick you up.

Cabin—Millset Trail

SAN ISABEL AREA

SNOWSLIDE TRAIL #1318

General description: Features nice views of the Snowslide and surrounding peaks, access to the Snowslide, and a car shuttle trip using the Greenhorn Mountain Road and the Cisneros Trail.

Option #1: *Elevation gain from CO 165:* 2,780'

    Elevations: Highest: 11,500' Lowest: 8,720'

    Miles (no side trips—one way): 5.7

Option #2: *Elevation gain from Lake Isabel:* 2,900'

    Elevations: Highest: 11,500' Lowest: 8,600'

    Miles (no side trips—one way): 6.2

Rating: Difficult

USGS topo map: San Isabel

Users: Motorcyclists, horses, hikers

Road directions: There are two access points for the Snowslide Trail from CO 165. One access point is on CO 165 9.1 miles north of the main turnoff to Rye, or 1.1 miles south of the turnoff to San Isabel. Parking is available on the east side of CO 165. The only sign is a "National Forest Land Welcome" sign at the fence opening. A second access point can be reached by driving into the recreation area at the Lake Isabel Work Center (San Isabel National Forest Ranger Station) 0.5 mile north of the CO 165 access point, or 0.6 mile south of the San Isabel turnoff. Continue 0.1 mile to a small parking area at a gated old logging road that is just before the entrance pay station. There is a trailhead sign. Concessionaires may try to assess a recreation area fee, but you do not need to pay it even though you are inside the area closure gate that is at CO 165.

    The Snowslide is a distinguishable landmark from the eastern plains in the Pueblo vicinity. The view of this landmark close-up makes the hike worthwhile. The **Snowslide Trail** from CO 165 begins with three switchbacks. At the third switchback, 0.3 mile up the trail, is a junction. The trail to the right (west-northwest) goes to the second trailhead at Lake Isabel and can be used if a Cisneros-Snowslide Trails loop is being done with one car available (see "Cisneros Trail"

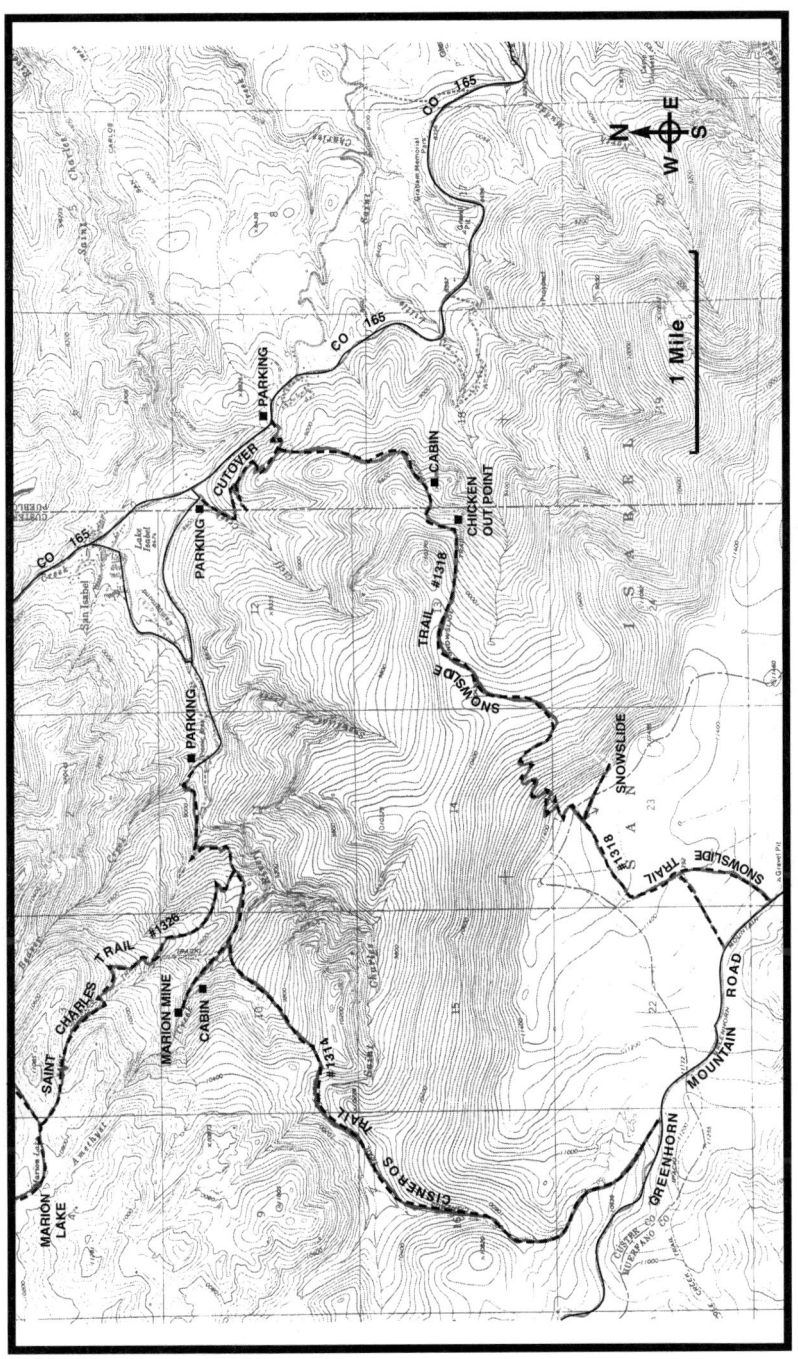

section). If you're using the trailhead at Lake Isabel, the trail starts up the old logging road along Cliff Creek. In 0.4 mile there is a signpost. Leave the road here to continue for another 0.4 mile on the Snowslide Trail to the junction.

Continuing from this junction, the remnants of an old cabin sit beside the trail at Mile 1.5 from the CO 165 trailhead. At Mile 1.8 is Chicken Out Point, where hikers are allowed to chicken out because of the steepness of the trail. There's a nice view of the Snowslide from here.

The trail continues to be steep for another 0.5 mile beyond Chicken Out Point. A welcome level stretch then lets you catch your breath before 11 switchbacks bring you to the top at a meadow. There are nice views of Saint Charles Peak, Scraggy Peaks, and Pikes Peak from this meadow.

The Snowslide is not visible once you reach the top but is about 0.3 mile to the east. Continue on the Snowslide Trail, which turns east (left) once you've reached the top. In a few yards the trail turns southwest to head for the middle of the meadow. At this turn it seems logical to bushwhack along the edge of the ridge until the Snowslide is reached, but too much downed timber eliminates that possibility. Instead, follow the Snowslide Trail southwest a few yards to a trail junction in the middle of the meadow, marked by a pole. This junction occurs before Snowslide Trail, still heading southwest, goes through an open gate in a fence line.

To reach the Snowslide, take the trail heading east-southeast (left), following the snowmobile markers, to a gate in the fence line and go through the gate. A few feet beyond the fence line the snowmobile trail turns right (south). Don't follow the snowmobile trail but keep on an east-southeast course. There is a very marginal trail from here to the Snowslide, complete with very old blazes, metal tags, and plastic streamers to keep you on course. But it can still be tricky so pay close attention. Retrace your steps back to the pole in the meadow to continue the Snowslide Trail.

The Snowslide Trail continues southwest from the pole and after 0.5 mile turns southeast into a meadow with good views of the Sangre de Cristo Mountains. A sign blocks the old trail (a road) where it turned southwest in the meadow. If you're doing a loop with the Cisneros Trail, this old road can be followed on foot to Greenhorn Mountain Road, but it can be boggy if wet. All motorized vehicles must use the new trail. The new trail continues southeast to the trees from the road closure sign. The trail meanders through the trees, eventually turning southwest and becoming Forest Road 352. Stay on Forest Road 352 to Greenhorn Mountain Road.

Retrace your steps from the junction of Forest Road 352 and Greenhorn Mountain Road, or hike 0.3 mile northwest on Greenhorn Mountain Road to pick up the old trail that goes through the meadow back to the road closure sign. The loop through the meadow lengthens the round trip hiking distance by 0.1 mile. If you're doing the Snowslide-Cisneros Trails loop via the new trail through the trees, it's 0.5 mile farther than cutting through the meadow.

CISNEROS TRAIL #1314—
MARION MINE TRAIL AND SAINT CHARLES TRAIL ACCESS

General description: A trail that gives access to the Saint Charles Trail and the Marion Mine, and offers a loop trip using Greenhorn Mountain Road and Snowslide Trail.

Users: Motorcyclists, horses, hikers

Option #1: *Elevation gain from trailhead to Greenhorn Mountain Road:* 2,400'

Elevations: Highest: 11,100' Lowest: 8,840'

Miles (one way): 4.9

Rating: Moderate

USGS topo map: San Isabel

Option #2: *Elevation gain, Cisneros and Snowslide Trails loop (two cars):* 2,800'

Elevations: Highest: 11,500' Lowest: 8,720'

Miles (for loop): 12

Rating: Moderate to difficult

USGS topo map: San Isabel

Road directions: The Cisneros, Marion Mine, and Saint Charles Trails begin as the same trail from the campground/picnic area at Lake Isabel. Signs refer to it as the Cisneros Trail. To reach the trailhead, drive northwest of Rye on CO 165, either 9.6 miles to the Lake Isabel Work Center (San Isabel National Forest Ranger Station) or 10.2 miles to San Isabel. During the summer, when the recreation facilities are open, use the access at the work center and drive along the south shore of Lake Isabel for 1.0 mile to its junction with the road to Saint Charles Campground, the group picnic site, and the trailhead. Take this road 0.7 mile to the end, where parking and restroom facilities are available. Lake Isabel Recreation Area is a U.S. Fee Area requiring in 2003 a $4.00 per vehicle day-use permit. Holders of Golden Age and Access Passports pay half the required fee.

If the facilities are closed, use the San Isabel approach on the north shore and drive 0.25 mile to the parking lot at the exit end of the one-way road. Hike up the one-way road for 0.75 mile to the junction mentioned above, where you can continue to the trailhead. If you hike on the road from the north shore parking lot, you'll need to add 1.5 miles and 280' elevation gain to your outing.

It's unfortunate that these roads are closed to vehicular traffic for most of the year, but vandalism of the facilities has left the concessionaire no choice. In good snow years the roads are used for cross-country skiing.

The **Cisneros Trail** begins along Beaver Creek but quickly leaves it to cross the ridge above the group picnic area. In 0.3 mile from the trailhead, the trail will be beyond the group site and at a former parking area. Cross the parking area to the trail. In another 0.3 mile the trail forks. The right fork, which climbs very steeply, has been blocked by logs to discourage its use. Follow the left fork through a switchback to the next turn in the trail at the bottom of a meadow peppered with a few trees. The top of the steep trail (also blocked by logs) comes in from the right at the bottom of this meadow. Continue up the trail through the meadow, watching for the Saint Charles Trail to the right near the top of the meadow, 0.75 mile from the trailhead. It's an easy trail to miss, but a small sign tacked to a tree ten yards up the trail will confirm it as the Saint Charles Trail (see "Saint Charles Trail" section). If you look back down the trail from near the junction of the Saint Charles and Cisneros Trails, Lake Isabel is visible.

The Cisneros Trail and Marion Mine Trail continue as the same trail for another 0.5 mile beyond the Saint Charles Trail junction. The Cisneros and Marion Mine Trails junction is obvious. The trail to the right (straight ahead) continues to the Marion Mine (see "Marion Mine Trail" section). The Cisneros Trail goes to the left, crosses Amethyst Creek, then climbs steeply for the next mile to a saddle at 10,180'. At the saddle you begin a 140' descent needed to reach the Saint Charles River. About 0.3 mile down from the saddle is an intermittent creek. A few remnants from a plane crash are just a few yards up this creek.

Once across Saint Charles River, a trail forks off to the right (west). This is an old road (now used by snowmobilers), which heads west for 1.5 miles, mostly through open meadow, to Greenhorn Mountain Road. You can make a loop trip by hiking 2.5 miles up the road (south) to the upper end of the Cisneros Trail.

Continue on the Cisneros Trail, watching for a willow meadow to the west at about 1.0 mile beyond Saint Charles River. In another 0.2 mile the trail crosses the creek. Make note of this area for the return trip. It's easy to miss this crossing and find yourself in the middle of the willows on a section of old trail. There is a short boggy section in the willows, but the trail can be followed for about 0.5 mile down the west side of the creek before downed timber forces you to cross back to the east side and the main trail.

After another 0.75 mile from the creek crossing, the trail goes through a fence line. Please close the gate behind you if it was closed. Once through the gate, bear right to pick up the trail again. Greenhorn Mountain Road is another 0.25 mile from the fence line.

The Cisneros Trail can be followed another 5.0 miles to Turkey Creek Road by hiking 0.3 mile (southeast) up Greenhorn Mountain Road, where the trail continues on the other side of the road. From this junction of the Cisneros Trail and Greenhorn Mountain Road, the trail drops 2,050' to Turkey Creek Road. Since Turkey Creek Road is almost 10 miles from the trailhead at Lake Isabel, it's not a good option for a day hike unless you have someone to pick you up at Turkey Creek Road.

Once at Greenhorn Mountain Road, a nice option if two cars are available is to hike 1.4 miles (southeast) along Greenhorn Mountain Road to Snowslide Trail #1318 (see "Snowslide Trail" section). At Mile 5.4 on the Snowslide Trail from Greenhorn Mountain Road (1.5 miles below Chicken Out Point), turn right (east-southeast) at the trail junction. Continue 0.3 mile to the trailhead on CO 165 (1.1 miles south of San Isabel).

If only one car is available, but this option is selected, it is another 2.3 miles back to your car via CO 165 and the road along the south side of Lake Isabel. A second option, if only one car is available, avoids CO 165 by going left (west-northwest) at the Mile 5.4 junction. The cutover trail reaches the road on the south shore of Lake Isabel in 0.8 mile. It is then another 1.6 miles back to your car via the road along the south shore of Lake Isabel.

MARION MINE TRAIL

General description: A popular hike to the remnants of an old zinc, lead, copper, and silver mine.

Elevation gain: 760'

Elevations: Highest: 9,600' Lowest: 8,840'

Miles (round trip): 3.1

Rating: Easy

USGS topo map: San Isabel

Users: Motorcyclists, horses, hikers

    The well-worn trail to the **Marion Mine** is actually the remnants of an old road. Refer to the "Cisneros Trail #1314—Marion Mine Trail and Saint Charles Trail Access" section for more information. Follow the Cisneros Trail, passing the Saint Charles Trail junction and leaving the Cisneros Trail at 1.25 miles from the trailhead. Once the Cisneros Trail and Marion Mine Trail junction is reached, the mine is only 0.3 mile farther. About halfway between this junction and the mine there is an old cabin. The cabin and the mine are located below rocky outcrops that can be seen for the last 0.3 mile of the trail. The trail is quite rocky near the cabin and the mine, so watch your step.

    The Marion Mine ruins are on private property, so take only pictures and leave only footprints as you explore this area. If you take children watch them closely, especially at the mine, as the rotten wood piles and boards are full of nails. A delightful place for a picnic is just above the mine, where there are two nice waterfalls and pools. Amethyst Creek can be bushwhacked to Marion Lake, but it's not for the faint of heart as some rock scrambling is required. A much easier way to get to Marion Lake is on the Saint Charles Trail (see "Saint Charles Trail" section).

Miner's cabin in summer—Marion Mine Trail

Miner's cabin in winter—Marion Mine Trail

Amethyst Creek waterfall at Marion Mine—Marion Mine Trail

SAINT CHARLES TRAIL #1326
(WITH SIDE TRIP TO MARION LAKE)

General description: A popular trail with three trailheads, good views, and options to climb Saint Charles Peak and/or hike to Marion Lake.

Users: Motorcyclists, horses, hikers, backpackers

Option #1: *Elevation gain to Marion Lake (only):* 2,040'

Elevation gain (return trip): 140'

Elevations: Highest: 10,880' Lowest: 8,840'
Elevation at Marion Lake: 10,740'

Miles (round trip): 7

Rating: Moderate

USGS topo map: San Isabel

Option #2: *Elevation gain to Saint Charles Peak from San Isabel trailhead:* 3,204'

Elevations: Highest: 11,784' Lowest: 8,840'

Miles (from San Isabel trailhead to CO 165): 11.5

Rating: Difficult

USGS topo maps: Saint Charles Peak, San Isabel

Option #3: *Elevation gain to Saint Charles Peak from CO 165:* 2,704'

Elevations: Highest: 11,784' Lowest: 9,080'

Miles (round trip): 10

Rating: Moderate to difficult

USGS topo map: Saint Charles Peak

The **Saint Charles Trail** is an 11.5-mile-long trail with a trailhead at the Lake Isabel Recreation Area (see "Cisneros Trail #1314—Marion Mine Trail and Saint Charles Trail Access" section), a trailhead on CO 165, 4.0 miles north of San Isabel, and a trailhead off Greenhorn Mountain Road (see "Ophir Creek—Bigelow Divide Area: Saint Charles Trail from Ophir Creek Road" section). From San Isabel to CO 165 makes a nice day hike if two cars are

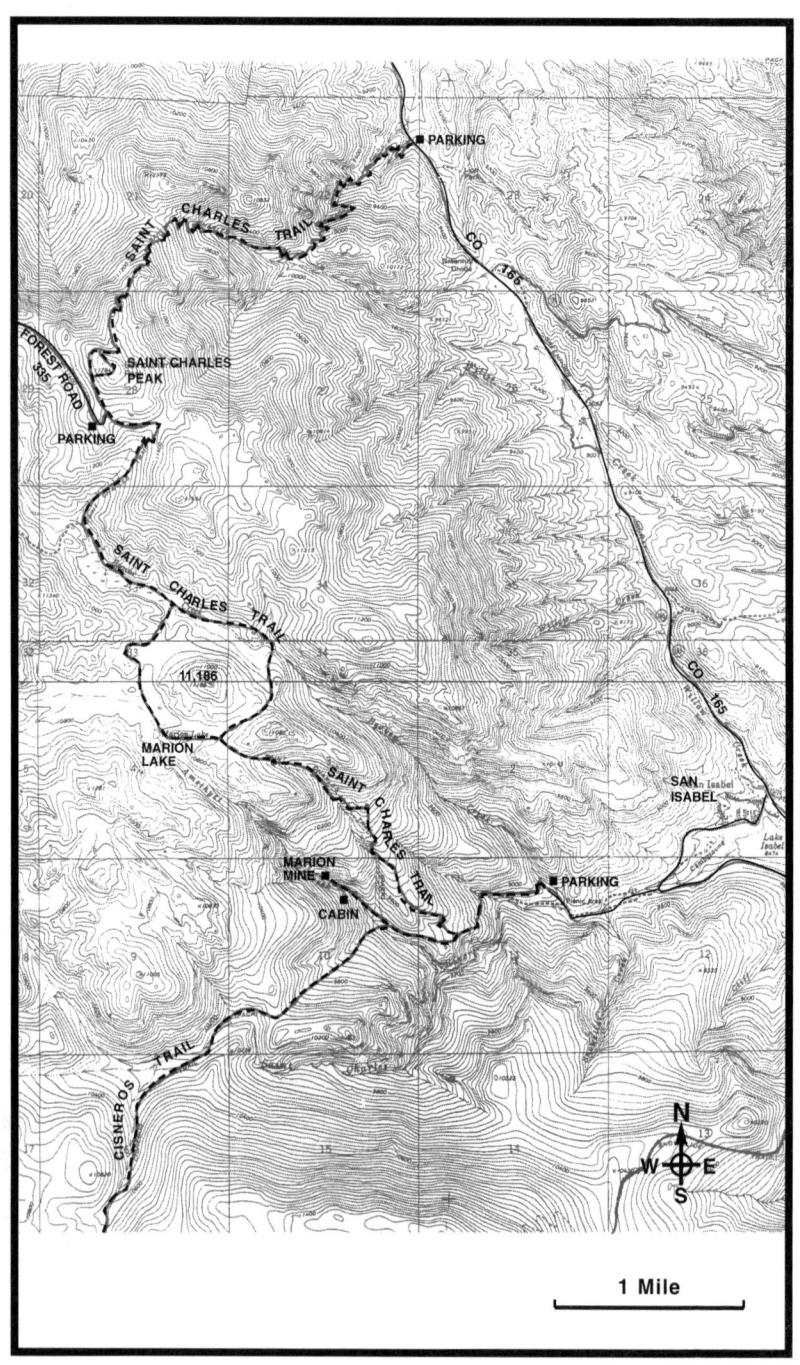

available for a shuttle. If only one car is available and Saint Charles Peak is your destination, the route from CO 165 is preferred over the longer route from San Isabel. Parking is available for this section of the trail on the east side of CO 165.

If the hike is begun on the Cisneros Trail at Lake Isabel, it is 6.5 miles to Saint Charles Peak. Even though the Saint Charles Trail can be hard to find where it exits the Cisneros Trail, once found it is a good trail, but it has a few steep sections.

At Mile 2.25 from the Cisneros Trail and Saint Charles Trail junction, the trail goes through a fence line to a saddle. Just after reaching the saddle, there is a side trail to the left (west) that leads to Marion Lake in 0.5 mile. Note that this side trail is only a two- to three-minute hike beyond the fence line. An uprooted signpost with sign may be found either on the ground or leaning against a tree at the trail junction.

Marion Lake is a nice destination if peak bagging doesn't appeal to you. To reach the lake, follow this side trail for 0.2 mile through the trees. When it reaches the willows it can be a bit wet underfoot. Watch for a large boulder in the middle of the meadow at a rocky outcrop. A few feet west of the boulder is a good place to cross to the north side of the meadow. The trail then continues west, passing the remnants of an old sawmill. Once at the meadow, which runs

Remnants of old sawmill near Marion Lake—Saint Charles Trail side trip

northwest and southeast, staying close to the right side helps keep the feet a bit drier as you head northwest to reach the dam and lake. There is fishing and camping if you don't mind sharing the area with cattle. Take time to explore the remains of the old buildings, the machinery, and the dam.

Marion Lake—Saint Charles Trail side trip

If you're bypassing Marion Lake and staying on the Saint Charles Trail, in 0.25 mile from the lake junction the trail will crest at 10,900', then drop 260' to the Beaver Creek crossing. Once across Beaver Creek, the trail crosses a small side creek which drains a gully and meadow to the north. The trail continues west and, after a few switchbacks through the trees, crosses a small ridge before returning to the meadow through which Beaver Creek flows.

Continue northwest in this beautiful meadow for 0.5 mile, where you will note a meadow to the south that heads over a low ridge. This meadow gives access to Marion Lake from the north. If you leave the Saint Charles Trail here (there's no official trail) and cross Beaver Creek (find the driest route possible), you can pick up a trail that follows the west side of this meadow and reaches Marion Lake in 0.9 mile. This trail makes a nice alternate route if you plan to retrace your steps from Saint Charles Peak.

Or, if Marion Lake is your only goal, the 2.8-mile loop around the 11,186' cone-shaped peak adds more interest to the hike. If you're making the loop counterclockwise and you reach a muddy section of the Saint Charles Trail with a log boardwalk, you're about 0.1 mile northwest of the best Beaver Creek crossing to reach the alternate trail to Marion Lake. Doing the loop counterclockwise is recommended because of the soggy trails around Marion Lake. That will make fewer miles to hike with wet boots.

But if the peak is your goal, continue from the log boardwalk on the Saint Charles Trail for another 0.7 mile to a junction with an old road. The road, which is in disuse, eventually reaches Greenhorn Mountain Road. The Saint Charles Trail (right fork) continues northeast. After 1.0 mile there is another junction. The left fork is the Saint Charles Trail access from Greenhorn Mountain Road via Ophir Creek Road. From this junction continue west-northwest (right fork) over a low, open ridge. The trail turns north and re-enters the trees for a short distance.

The Saint Charles Trail does not actually cross the top of the peak, but rather skirts the west side of the peak about 100' below the top. When the trail breaks out into an open meadow, hike to the middle of the open area, then leave the trail, hiking east to reach the top of Saint Charles Peak. If you wish, you can continue along the trail until it turns east, where there is an old hitching post on the left side of the trail. From the hitching post, hike southeast to the top of the peak. The meadow on top of Saint Charles Peak is beautiful, with some great views of the surrounding mountains, plains, and valleys.

If you're continuing to CO 165, the trail descends in 5.0 miles to the trailhead by a series of switchbacks. Hike northwest off the summit to the hitching post to pick up the trail. From the hitching post the trail heads east for 0.1 mile, then turns north following a ridge, first through the forest and then through an open area to a small, rocky outcrop with good views. The descent continues by switchbacks, re-entering the trees at 11,480'. After more switchbacks the trail reaches a pass at 10,800', where it turns east and descends with more switchbacks to a saddle at 10,050'. The trail continues in a northeasterly direction with more switchbacks, a couple of creek crossings, and another ridge walk before reaching CO 165.

SAN CARLOS TRAIL #1320 AND NATURAL ARCH

General description: A trail with two trailheads that crosses the Saint Charles River (a great place for a picnic and some fishing); or you can follow the Little Saint Charles Creek to a natural arch.

Elevation loss from CO 78 to Saint Charles River: 850'

Elevations: Highest at trailhead parking on CO 78: 8,163'
Lowest at Saint Charles River: 7,360'

Miles (one way): 1.5

Rating: Easy

USGS topo maps: Saint Charles, San Isabel

Users: Motorcyclists, horses, hikers, fishermen

Road directions for CO 78 trailhead: This trailhead is off the dirt portion of CO 78 running between Beulah and CO 165. Check your odometer so you can clock the miles. From the main entrance to Pueblo Mountain Park in Beulah, drive 4.4 miles west on CO 78. Or, from San Isabel, drive 3.2 miles north on CO 165 to the CO 78 junction, then follow CO 78 east for 5.5 miles. A small parking area and a sign are at the trailhead.

The **San Carlos Trail** from CO 78 begins as a former forest road, heading south and descending 45' to a small creek crossing in 0.25 mile. Continue to follow the road for another 0.25 mile. At this point the road has been blocked off for restoration. A sign marks the trail as it leaves the road and turns south. From this sign it is 1.0 mile down to the Saint Charles River. This section of the trail has views of the Snowslide and Greenhorn Mountain. Just before reaching Saint Charles River, the trail crosses Willis Creek. There's no bridge, but several rocks will keep you high and dry. A bridge crosses Saint Charles River.

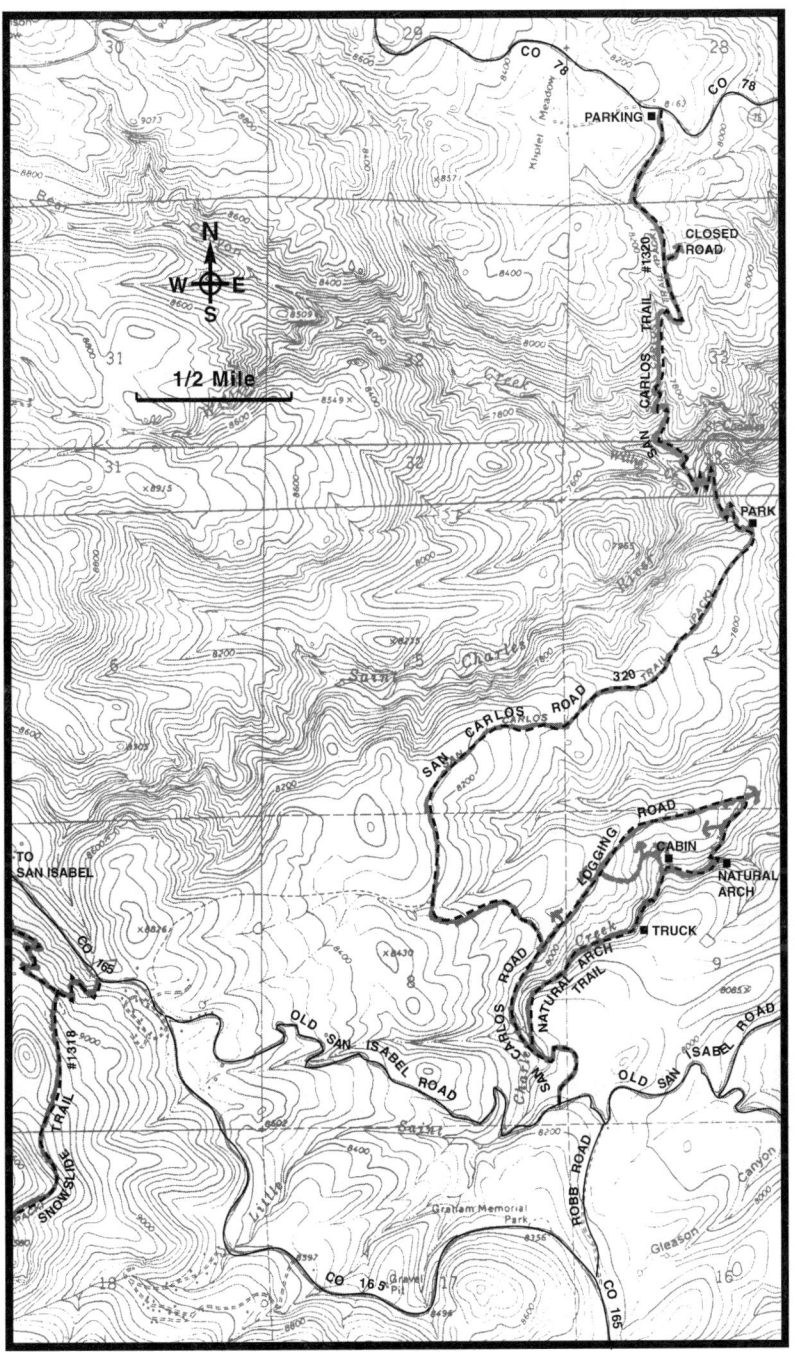

Elevation loss from Old San Isabel Road to Saint Charles River: 1,100' (approximately)

Elevations: Highest: 8,260'   Lowest at Saint Charles River: 7,360' Elevation at junction of Old San Isabel Road and San Carlos Road 320: 8,160'

Miles (from Old San Isabel Road to Saint Charles River—one way): 3.6

Rating: Easy to moderate

USGS topo maps: Saint Charles, San Isabel

Users: Motorcyclists, horses, hikers, fishermen

Road directions for Old San Isabel Road trailhead: From the main entrance to Rye, drive north on CO 165 6.4 miles to Robb Road. It's helpful to watch for the YMCA Camp Jackson turnoff, which is 1.4 miles south of Robb Road. Follow Robb Road 0.6 mile downhill to its intersection with Old San Isabel Road. Turn left (northwest) onto Old San Isabel Road and follow it for 0.2 mile to San Carlos Road 320. To reach this point from San Isabel, drive 1.4 miles south on CO 165 to the north end of Old San Isabel Road. Follow Old San Isabel Road 2.1 miles to San Carlos Road 320.

If you have a car, leave it near the cattleguard at the junction of San Carlos Road 320 and Old San Isabel Road. A high-clearance 4-wheel-drive vehicle can continue 0.3 mile down to the Little Saint Charles Creek, where the road crosses the creek and continues for 2.8 miles to San Carlos Trail #1320. Be watching for a signpost (no sign) that marks the trailhead. There is a small parking area on the right side of the road. If you miss the trailhead, the road ends 0.5 mile beyond the trailhead. San Carlos Road can be very muddy and slick when wet. You'll need to open and close a couple of gates. This is an access road only, so stay on the road.

The **San Carlos Trail** descends 320' in 0.5 mile by several switchbacks to the Saint Charles River. If you're hiking on San Carlos Road, be aware that the road has its ups and downs, literally, as it negotiates meadows, drainages, and ridges.

Elevation loss to natural arch from Little Saint Charles Creek crossing: 400'

Elevations: At the junction of Little Saint Charles Creek and San Carlos Road 320: 8,000'   At arch: 7,600'

Miles (round trip along creek): 2.5
  (round trip via logging roads): 3

Rating: Easy

USGS topo map: San Isabel

Users: Hikers, fishermen

An interesting side trip from San Carlos Road 320 is to hike to the **natural arch** that is on the Little Saint Charles Creek. The Little Saint Charles Creek does not flow through the arch. In fact, the arch is above the creek on the east (south) side and is turned sideways to the current flow of the creek. It can be challenging finding the arch, but exploring this natural phenomenon is well worth the effort.

If you've driven down to the Little Saint Charles Creek, park near the bridge crossing. There are two ways to reach the arch. One is by hiking down the Little Saint Charles Creek. The other uses a series of old logging roads.

The creek crossings generally are not a problem. The real challenge comes from rock scrambles and brush along the creek. To hike via the creek, start on its east side. The first 0.3 mile is a decent trail due to fishermen use, but thereafter it can be a real scramble. The trail gets lost in overgrowth and rock walls. The creek must be crossed a dozen times or more, depending on your route choice. It can take more than an hour hiking along the creek to reach the arch. It can be very frustrating, but the nice fishing holes and small waterfalls along the way are sure to delight any cranky hiker.

The challenge with the logging road route is the numerous roads on the ridge. For this route, cross the bridge and hike 0.4 mile up the hill (away from the creek) on San Carlos Road 320 to a side road leading off to the northeast. At this point San Carlos Road 320 begins to top out and turns left (north). Follow the side road. About 100' up this side road is a mound of dirt across the road, preventing vehicular traffic. Several of these earthen dams will be encountered, with a path around each. The trail has been partially marked with orange tagging and a few cairns.

At the third earth dam, the road goes down a small hill to a fork. Take the right fork. Please note that the left fork, which heads north, is grass-covered and could be easily missed. The next fork, about 0.2 mile farther, is in the middle of a grassy meadow. Again, take the right fork. At the far edge of the meadow is another fork. Take the more traveled road to the left. The road to the right goes down to the remains of an old cabin by the Little Saint Charles Creek and makes a nice side trip.

Continuing 0.6 mile on the left fork from the grassy meadow, you can see the confluence of the Little Saint Charles Creek (right) with an intermittent stream coming in from the left. Be watching for a road to the right. A cairn and a small old tree stump in the grass are on the right side of the road just before this junction. If you should miss it and continue heading straight down the ridge, the main road ends in 0.1 mile at a nice view, into the Little Saint Charles Creek canyon. For a better view, hike another 100' through the scrub oak beyond the end of the road. Then reverse your steps back up the hill (about a 3-minute hike) to the first road to your left. As you start down the road it curves to the right (southwest) and begins to descend the hill. Follow this road 0.1 mile to the next fork and go left. Hike down the hill to a grassy area where the road ends. North Peak is visible to the south. The arch can be seen below to the southeast.

When the road ends in the grassy area, keep heading straight down the hill toward the creek to a second grassy area just below a few trees and bushes. There's a pine tree in the middle of this grassy patch. Continue down the left side of this area until you pick up the trail. The trail is faint in places, but it is tagged and has cairns. You'll need to make one creek crossing to stand at the base of the arch using this route.

SOUTH CREEK TRAIL #1321

This trail begins in Lion Park off CO 165 and descends to Pueblo Mountain Park in Beulah (see "Beulah Area: Pueblo Mountain Park Trails and South Creek Trail" sections).

WACHOB TRAIL #1319

General description: A short trail that ends with a scenic overlook of Lake Isabel and San Isabel.

Elevation gain: 200'

Elevations: Highest: 9,240' Lowest: 9,040'

Miles (round trip): 2

Rating: Easy

USGS topo maps: Saint Charles Peak, San Isabel

Users: Hikers, cross-country skiers

Road directions: Wachob Trail can be reached by driving 1.25 miles north of San Isabel on CO 165 to the Boy Scout Camp turnoff (Forest Road 380). Drive 0.5 mile up Forest Road 380 to its junction with Forest Road 317. Park along Forest Road 317, which makes a 0.2-mile loop. Walk back to the intersection of Forest Roads 380 and 317, where the trail begins heading south-southeast.

Wachob Trail is a delightful trail that runs along the top of a broad, tree-covered ridge. The trail was named after John "Jack" Alvin Wachob, Jr. Jack worked for the Forest Service at San Isabel for 21 years, and was asked by his supervisor to find three areas that would be suitable for a family outing in both summer and winter. This area was chosen from the three selections, and the trail was built in the late 1970s. The trail was named for Jack when he retired in 1980. The trail is a nice tribute to a man who had opportunities to work elsewhere but who chose to stay at San Isabel because of the beauty of the area. He died in 1983 at age 64.

This trail is an easy cross-country ski trail, so it never gets steep. Spend time enjoying the view from the scenic overlook at the end of the trail.

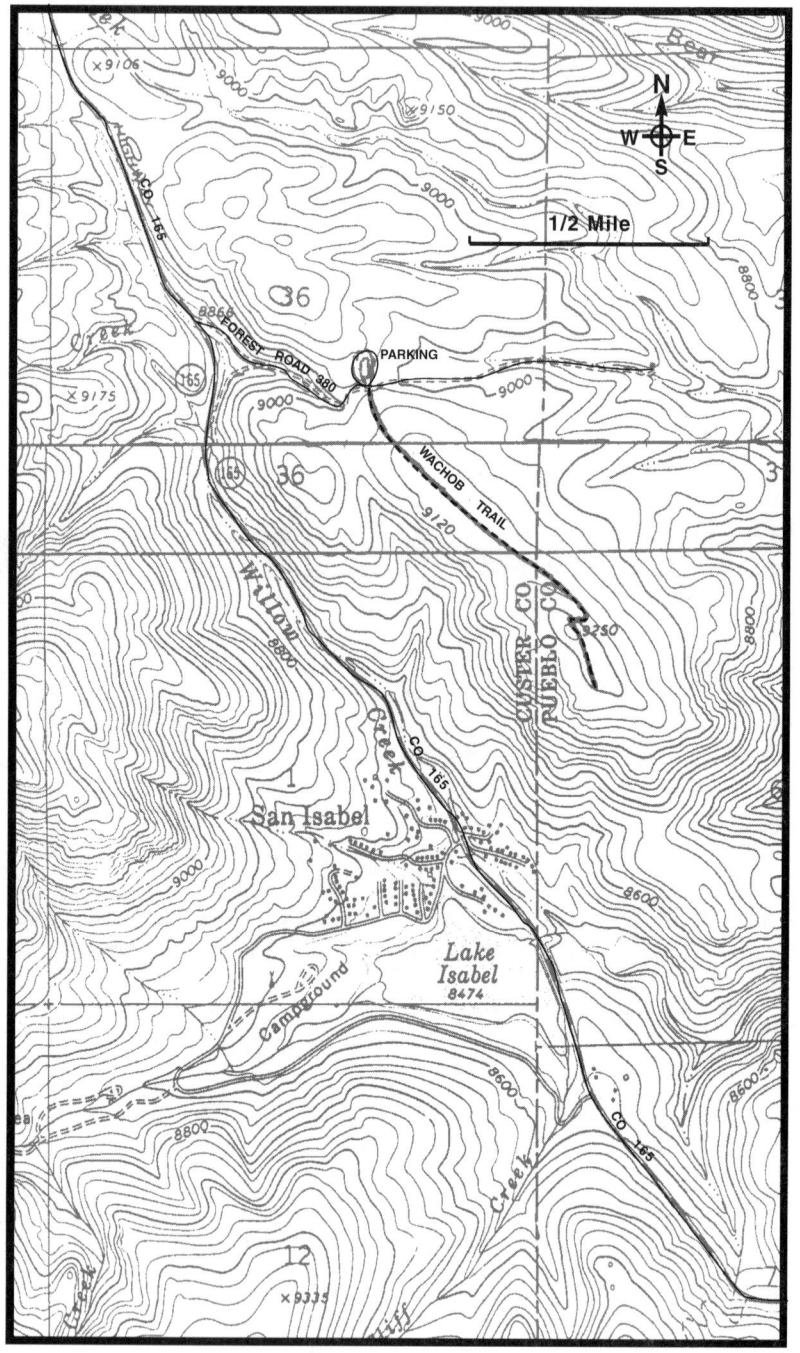

WALSENBURG AREA

HOGBACK TRAIL

General description: A loop trail in a state park that leads to the top of a hogback ridge with good views.

Elevation gain: 80'

Elevations: Highest: 6,560'   Lowest: 6,480'

Miles (round trip): 1.5

Rating: Easy

Map: Area map obtained at Visitor Center

Users: Hikers

Road directions: Hogback Trail is within Lathrop State Park, so an entrance fee is required. From the junction of Business I-25 and CO 160 in Walsenburg, drive 3.3 miles west on CO 160 to the entrance to Lathrop State Park. Stop at the Visitor Center for a map and to pay the necessary fees. Drive around the east end of Martin Lake to the north side of the lake. Trailhead parking is opposite the Rock Outcrop day-use area.

The **Hogback Trail** forms a loop that leads to the top of the hogback ridge to the north, where the views of Martin Lake, Horseshoe Lake, and the Spanish Peaks make it worth carrying a camera. From the ridge, Greenhorn Mountain is visible to the north. Dogs are allowed on the trail, but must be kept on a leash no longer than six feet. The area offers fishing, camping, water-skiing, sailing, wind surfing, and swimming (dogs are not allowed on the swim beaches). This high-plains grassland dotted with piñon and juniper trees became Colorado's first state park in 1962.

A sign at the trailhead gives an overview of the trail. If you've not previously hiked the trail, hiking it counterclockwise is best. When the trail seems to end, it is marked by posts with an arrow to give directions.

A rocky outcropping, near Loops A & B in Piñon Campground, is 0.25 mile up the trail. Take some time to explore these fascinating sandstone boulders. Various trails from the campground lead to this rock formation.

The loop trail leaves the sandstone boulders, heading toward the hogback. As the trail zigzags up the side of the ridge the views get better, but watch your step, as the trail is rocky in places. Before beginning its descent the trail follows the hogback, heading west for 0.2 mile.

MARTIN LAKE TRAIL

General description: A loop trail around Martin Lake offering a bit of peace, enhanced by flowers, birds, and deer.

Elevation gain: None

Elevation: 6,480'

Miles (round trip): 2.5

Rating: Easy

Map: Area map obtained at Visitor Center

Users: Hikers, bikers, horses

Road directions: Follow the directions to Lathrop State Park described in the "Hogback Trail" section. From within the park, the Martin Lake Trail can be accessed from several areas, including the Visitor Center, the day-use areas and the nearby campgrounds.

The **Martin Lake Trail** encircles Martin Lake, which is one of the two lakes within Lathrop State Park. No motorized vehicles are allowed on the trail, so it offers great opportunities to view birds, deer and other wildlife.

WETMORE AREA

LEWIS CREEK—HIGHLINE TRAIL #1331

General description: Features a delightful creek in the spring and good views from higher elevations; continues as a backcountry road utilized by many outdoor recreationists.

Option #1: *Elevation gain from Lewis Creek Trail parking area to Forest Road 315:* 3,020'

    Elevations: Highest: 9,920' Lowest: 6,900'

    Miles (round trip): 10

    Rating: Difficult

    USGS topo maps: Hardscrabble Mountain, Wetmore

    Users: Motorcyclists, horses, hikers

Option #2: *Elevation gain from CO 96 to Adobe Peak via Lewis Creek Trail:* 3,500'

    Elevations: Highest: 10,188' Lowest: 6,691'

    Miles (round trip): 13.5

    Rating: Difficult

    USGS topo maps: Hardscrabble Mountain, Wetmore

    Users: Motorcyclists, horses, hikers

Road directions: From the junction of CO 96 and CO 67 in Wetmore, drive west on CO 96, 3.2 miles to the Lewis Creek Trail access road (Forest Road 310). A parking area is 0.4 mile from the highway. If you have a low-clearance vehicle, use caution while negotiating this access road.

In the first 2.0 miles you'll gain 1,100' elevation as the **Lewis Creek Trail** meanders across Lewis Creek, which has some delightful little waterfalls when there is water in it. In the next 1.0 mile, using two sets of switchbacks, you'll gain another 1,000' elevation. There are some nice views from the first set of switchbacks. At 0.75 mile beyond the switchbacks, the trail levels out and goes through a grassy aspen meadow with views of the Scraggy Peaks to the southeast. In crossing this meadow you may have to negotiate some downed aspen.

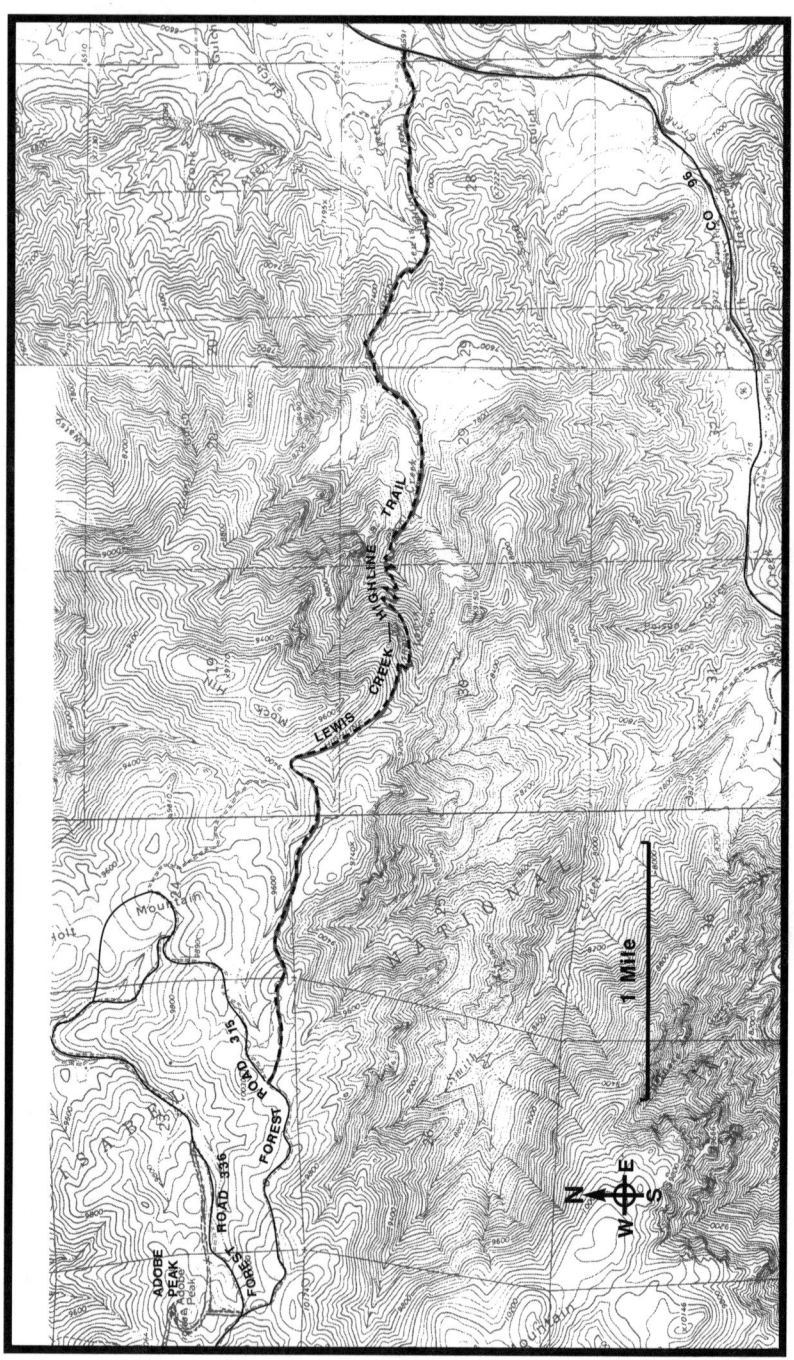

From the meadow it is another 1.25 miles to Forest Road 315, with views of Greenhorn Mountain, Saint Charles Peak, Deer Peak, and the Scraggy Peaks.

If you care to hike 1.1 miles west on Forest Road 315, you will reach the junction with Forest Road 336 at the base of Adobe Peak. The summit of Adobe Peak is 0.25 mile straight north of this junction.

Lewis Creek Trail is part of the Highline Trail, which can be followed to Oak Creek Campground via Forest Roads 315, 336, and 274, and the Lion Canyon Trail (see "Cañon City Area: Lion Canyon—Highline Trail" section). From the junction of Forest Roads 315 and 336 at the base of Adobe Peak, turn northwest on Forest Road 336. At the junction of Forest Roads 336 and 274, turn north on Forest Road 274.

Watch for the junction of Forest Roads 274 and 304. From this junction continue 2.6 miles north on Forest Road 274, through a big meadow, to a gate, which is in the trees. The road emerges into another beautiful meadow 0.1 mile north of this gate. This is Locke Park. Once in Locke Park continue for another 0.3 mile, where a post marks an obscure road to the left (west). Take this road 0.2 mile (keep left when it forks—the right fork is a snowmobile route) to the Lion Canyon Trail, which begins near the big shady pine at the edge of the meadow. If you reach a second gate in Locke Park, you are 0.25 mile beyond the post and obscure road; retrace your steps.

It is 18.25 miles from CO 96 to the Oak Creek Campground, so excellent physical condition is necessary, along with someone to pick you up at the other end. Hiking 10.0 miles on a road doesn't offer much appeal to most people, but it is mentioned for the very ambitious.

Option #3: *Elevation gain from junction of Forest Roads 271/274 to Adobe Peak via Forest Roads 274 and 336:* 1,675'

    Elevations: Highest: 10,188' Lowest: 8,513'

    Miles (one way): 5.25

    Rating: Moderate

    USGS topo map: Hardscrabble Mountain

    Users: High-clearance vehicles, motorcyclists, horses, mountain bikers, hikers, snowmobilers, and cross-country skiers

Option #4: *Elevation gain from junction of Forest Roads 271/274 via Forest Roads 274/304 to junction of Forest Roads 304/271 (cross-country ski shuttle):* 1,300'

Elevations: Highest: 9,800'
At junction of Forest Roads 271/274: 8,513'
Lowest at junction of Forest Roads 304/271: 8,000'

Miles (one way): 10

Rating: Moderate

USGS topo maps: Curley Peak, Hardscrabble Mountain, Mount Tyndall, Rockvale

Users: High-clearance vehicles, motorcyclists, horses, mountain bikers, hikers, snowmobilers, and cross-country skiers

More road directions: In addition to the USGS topo maps, a recent San Isabel National Forest map is highly recommended for exploring the roads, trails, and peaks in this area. The Highline Trail can also be reached from Forest Road 271. From McKenzie Junction (CO 96 and CO 165), drive 5.5 miles west on CO 96 to Forest Road 271. Follow Forest Road 271 for 5.6 miles to Forest Road 274. High-clearance vehicles are recommended on Forest Road 274, which climbs along Willow Creek, reaching Forest Road 336 in 2.8 miles. Forest Roads 274 and 336 at this junction are on the Highline Trail.

Forest Road 274 continues north 6.25 miles to Locke Park, while Forest Road 336 reaches the base of Adobe Peak and Forest Road 315 in 2.1 miles. If you plan to hike the Lewis Creek Trail from Forest Road 315, the trailhead is 1.1 miles along Forest Road 315 from its junction with Forest Road 336. There is a trailhead sign, but it is easy to miss since it is located off the roadway. Park at the trailhead or at the base of the 10,030' hill, which is 0.1 mile beyond the Lewis Creek trailhead.

Another access to the Highline Trail (Forest Road 274) is via Forest Road 304. From the junction of Forest Roads 271 and 274 (Willow Creek access), drive another 3.5 miles along Forest Road 271 to Forest Road 304. The latter road climbs steeply to the Highline Trail in 3.5 miles.

From its junction with Forest Road 304, Forest Road 271 continues north for 1.0 mile, where it ends at its junction with Fremont County Roads 66 and 143. Fremont County Road 143 (Oak Creek Grade Road) can be followed 16.5 miles to Cañon City.

NEWLIN CREEK TRAIL #1335

(see "Florence Area" section)

RUDOLPH MOUNTAIN TRAIL #1327

General description: Aspen trees along this trail make it a wondrous place in the fall if you're lucky enough to be there when the leaves are at peak color.

Elevation gain to Rudolph Mountain: 2,634'

Elevations: Highest: 10,334'   Lowest: 8,000'

Miles (one way): 4.25

Rating: Moderate to difficult

USGS topo maps: Deer Peak, Hardscrabble Mountain, Wetmore

Users: Hikers

Road directions: From the junction of CO 67 and CO 96 in Wetmore, drive 4.3 miles west on CO 96 to Forest Road 387. Follow Forest Road 387 for 3.5 miles to Forest Road 386. Then take Forest Road 386 for 2.6 miles to the trailhead parking area. If coming from McKenzie Junction (CO 165 and CO 96), drive 6.1 miles south on CO 165 to Forest Road 386. Or, from San Isabel, drive 12.3 miles north on CO 165 to Forest Road 386. Then follow Forest Road 386 for 3.0 miles to the trailhead. There is no trail sign and only limited parking.

Rudolph Mountain Trail begins up School Section Draw, following an overgrown road. At Mile 0.25 you'll pass an old foundation. A side trail just before the first creek crossing where the road ends (Mile 0.3) leads to another old foundation. The trail crosses the creek two more times, finally staying on the left side of the creek.

The mile after the third creek crossing has several switchbacks, and even then the trail is steep. Near the top a small concrete structure surrounds a small spring. Several sections of the trail beyond this point have become overgrown, but a few orange markers help to identify the trail. You may wish to take tagging material with you to further mark the trail.

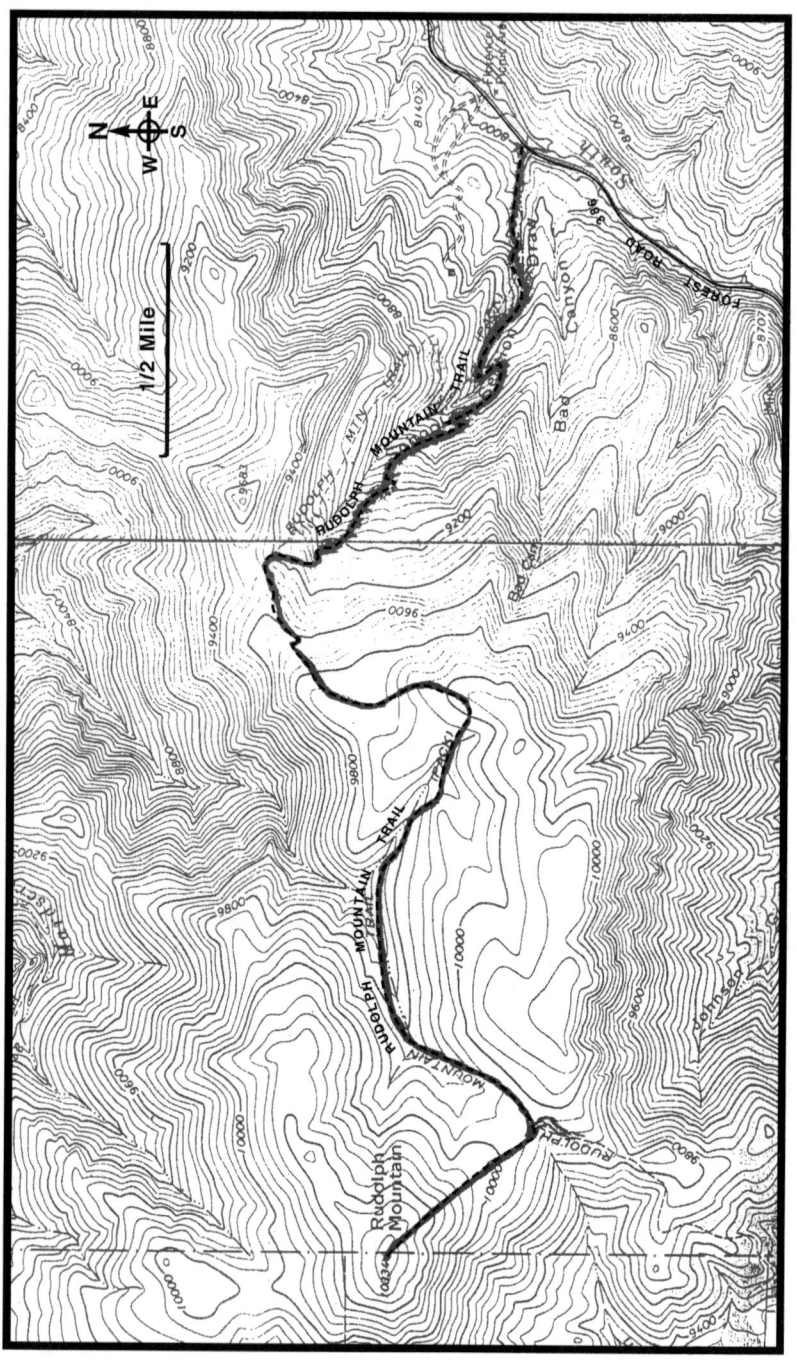

Once at the top of School Section Draw, the trail turns southwest and south, staying fairly level for the next 0.75 mile. The trail then crosses a ridge, turns west and northwest, and begins a 300' descent in 0.7 mile to another creek crossing. This section of trail has several downed trees, but they are easily bypassed.

As you exit the woods into the meadow after the creek crossing, note your location so you can pick up the trail again on the return trip. The trail through the meadow has become completely overgrown, but staying in the middle of the meadow and following various types of trail markers (mostly orange) makes fairly decent hiking. Continue to the south end of the meadow, where the trail intersects a 4-wheel-drive road.

The road to the left (east) descends through private property to CO 165. Do not go this way unless you have an emergency. The road to the right (west) leads to Rudolph Mountain. Follow the road through the meadow to the trees. The road ends, but a sparsely tagged route leads northwest up the hill, through the aspen, to a deteriorating fence line. Follow the fence line until it reaches its high point. Then cross the fence line and head west to the top of Rudolph Mountain. It's hard to say exactly where the top of Rudolph Mountain is located, but continue along the ridge, heading slightly downhill until you reach the western edge, for some good views and a nice place for lunch.

There is more than one way to reach the top of Rudolph Mountain, and therefore more than one way to descend. The top of Rudolph Mountain looks the same in all directions, so accurate compass bearings or a well-tagged trail are a must for getting safely off this mountain. Once you leave the road in the meadow, there is no official trail. You may wish to add additional tags that are clearly visible for the descent. Even experienced hikers can get confused trying to descend this mountain.

APPENDIX A

TEN ESSENTIALS AND OTHER USEFUL ITEMS

Everyone going into the backcountry should have the following items on **every** trip. Learn how to read a topographic map and use a compass. Take a first-aid course. Maps, compasses, and first-aid kits are useful only if you know how to use them.

- The appropriate map(s)
- A compass
- Sunglasses and sunscreen
- Extra clothing (always include raingear)
- Extra food
- A pocketknife
- Matches in a waterproof container
- A candle or other firestarter
- A flashlight with extra bulb and batteries
- A first-aid kit

In addition you'll want a <u>full</u> <u>water</u> <u>bottle</u>. All backcountry water, if available, must be treated before drinking. On a day hike it's easier and safer to take a sufficient supply from home. A minimum of one quart per person is recommended. On hot days plan to double that amount. On overnight trips take a water filter. It's also helpful to leave an extra water supply in your vehicle for your return. The water may be hot, but it's wet.

An <u>emergency</u> <u>blanket</u> (two ounces) or <u>bag</u> (three ounces) can be very effective in keeping a lost or injured victim warm and dry. The reflective nature of the aluminized material will retain most of the radiated body heat. Both give shelter from the wind. Unfolded, a blanket is 56" x 84" and a bag is 36" x 84". Collapsed, each is approximately 4 x 2.5 x 1.5 inches.

A mirror or a piece of tinfoil and a whistle are excellent <u>signaling devices</u>.

The following is a checklist of other equipment you may want to include in your daypack:

    lip balm

    facial tissue

    toilet paper

    bandana

    allergy medication

    notebook/pen

    insect repellent

    water germicidal tablets

    steel cup

    a piece of 1/8" nylon cord (about 12' long)

    camera/film/accessories

    binoculars

    Colorado Outdoor Recreation Search and Rescue Card

    fishing gear/license

    field guide

    orange vest (hunting season)

Don't forget to take your <u>hiking</u> <u>boots</u> and <u>socks</u> if you wear street shoes or sneakers in the car.

Recommended items for a <u>first-aid</u> <u>kit</u>:

- 6 one-inch bandaids
- 4 4 x 4-inch sterile gauze pads
- 4 2 x 3-inch sterile nonstick pads
- 1 large compress bandage (or sanitary napkin)
- 1 roll 2-inch x 5-yards gauze
- 1 roll cloth tape (0.5-inch wide)
- 1 roll adhesive tape (1-inch x 5-yards)
- Alcohol pads or small bottle isopropyl alcohol
- Antibiotic ointment
- Small bar of soap
- Moleskin
- 1 triangular bandage
- 1 elastic bandage
- 12 aspirin
- 6 antacid tablets
- Thermometer
- 6 safety pins (various sizes)
- Needle for splinters and ticks
- Scissors and tweezers if not included in your pocketknife
- Nailclippers with file
- Emergency/survival handbook
- Coins for phone

APPENDIX B

BACKPACKING EQUIPMENT

Besides the items listed in Appendix A, an overnight trip requires some obvious additional equipment, such as a sleeping bag, a tent, and cooking utensils. The following list gives suggestions of nice things to have. You may wish to develop your own checklist. It's not a pleasant experience to get deep into the backcountry and realize that you left an essential item at home.

Always camp at least 100 feet from water sources and trails.

Always use a checklist to make sure you have the necessary equipment.

Clothing
- Poncho
- Rain pants
- Windbreaker
- Down or polyester vest
- Wool sweater
- T-shirt
- Turtleneck
- Long pants
- Shorts
- Extra underwear
- Lightweight socks
- Wool hiking socks
- Long johns for sleeping
- Sleeping socks
- Sun hat
- Wool hat or earband
- Gloves
- Boots
- Camp shoes
- Bandana
- Swimsuit

Cooking
- Food (develop menu)
- Stove
- Fuel
- Funnel
- Matches
- Cleaning wire for stove
- Hot pads
- Can & bottle opener
- Cup
- Mess kit (plate/bowl)
- Pan/pot/fry lid/pot handle
- Cooking spoon
- Knife/spoon/fork
- Pancake turner
- Water filter
- Dish towel
- S.O.S soap pads
- Aluminum foil
- Grill
- Hotdog sticks
- Napkins
- Salt/Pepper

Sleeping
- Tent/fly
- Tent stakes/poles/guy lines
- Ground cloth
- Sleeping bag
- Sleeping pad
- Eyeglass case

Hauling
- Backpack
- Day or waist pack

Other Stuff
- Clothes pins (6) and line (nylon cord)
- Large garbage bag/extra plastic bags
- Rubber bands/twist ties
- Thread
- Folding saw/hatchet
- Accessory straps
- Alarm clock
- Wristwatch
- Car key

Toiletries
- Hand lotion
- Toothpaste
- Toothbrush
- Comb/brush
- Biodegradable soap
- Face cloth
- Deodorant
- Towel
- Facial tissue
- Biodegradable toilet paper

APPENDIX C

MAPS USED IN THIS GUIDE

Forest Service Maps

    Pike National Forest

    San Isabel National Forest

Web Site

    www.coloradolottery.com/about/trailmaps

Topographic Maps (7.5')

Badito Cone	McIntyre Hills
Beulah	Mount Big Chief
Cañon City	Mount Pittsburg
Cascade	Northwest Pueblo
Cooper Mountain	Phantom Canyon
Cripple Creek South	Rice Mountain
Curley Peak	Rockvale
Deer Peak	Royal Gorge
Hardscrabble Mountain	Rye
Hayden Butte	Saint Charles Peak
High Park	San Isabel
Hobson	Southwest Pueblo
Iron Mountain	Swallows
Manitou Springs	Wetmore

MAP SOURCES

Many sporting goods stores carry National Forest maps and USGS topographic maps. The yellow pages of your local telephone book list additional map sources. Forest Service offices carry the National Forest maps.

All Colorado topographic maps may be purchased over the counter or by mail order from:

>Branch of Distribution
>U.S. Geological Survey
>Federal Center
>Denver, CO 80225

APPENDIX D

INFORMATION SOURCES

Bureau of Land Management
Cañon City District Office
P.O. Box 2200
3170 East Main St.
Cañon City, CO 81212-2200
(719) 269-8500

Colorado Department of Local Affairs
CORSAR
222 South Sixth St., Room 409
Grand Junction, CO 81501
(970) 248-7310

Colorado Mountain Club
710 10th St., Suite 200
Golden, CO 80401
(303) 279-3080
(ask for El Pueblo Chapter contact and phone number)

Colorado State Division of Wildlife
600 Reservoir Rd.
Pueblo, CO 81005
(719) 561-5300

3170 East Main St.
Cañon City, CO 81212
(719) 269-8500

Department of Planning and Community Development
211 East D St.
Pueblo, CO 81003
(719) 543-6006

Dinosaur Depot
330 Royal Gorge Blvd. (4th & U.S. 50)
Cañon City, CO 81212
(719) 269-7150
(800) 987-6379

Division of Parks and Outdoor Recreation
640 Pueblo Reservoir Rd.
Pueblo, CO 81005
(719) 561-9320

Lathrop State Park
70 County Road 502
Walsenburg, CO 81089
(719) 738-2376

Mountain Park Environment Center
9161 Mountain Park Road
Beulah, CO 81023
(719) 485-4444

Pike and San Isabel National Forest Headquarters
2840 Kachina Drive
Pueblo, CO 81008
(719) 553-1400

District Offices:
Pikes Peak Ranger District
601 South Weber St.
Colorado Springs, CO 80903
(719) 636-1602

San Carlos Ranger District
3170 East Main St.
Cañon City, CO 81212
(719) 269-8500

Pueblo County Historical Society
Vail Hotel
217 South Grand
Pueblo, CO 81003
(719) 543-6772

Pueblo Greenway and Nature Center
5200 Nature Center Rd.
Pueblo, CO 81003
(719) 549-2414

Pueblo Library District
Western Research
100 East Abriendo Ave.
Pueblo, CO 81004
(719) 543-9601

Pueblo Parks and Recreation Department
800 Goodnight Ave.
Pueblo, CO 81005
(719) 566-1745

BIBLIOGRAPHY

American Red Cross. 1979. *Standard First Aid & Personal Safety*. Second Edition. American National Red Cross.

"Beaver Creek Wilderness Study Area." U.S. Bureau of Land Management Brochure and Map, Cañon City, CO.

Beulah Historical Society. 1979. *From Mace's Hole, the Way It Was, to Beulah, the Way It Is: A Comprehensive History of Beulah, CO.* (Colorado Springs, CO: Century One Press).

Boddie, Caryn and Peter. 1984. *The Hiker's Guide to Colorado*. (Helena, MT: Falcon Press).

Boody, Carol J. 1989. *A Mountain Bike Tour Guide for Cañon City, Colorado*. (Cañon City, CO: Master Printers).

Carmak, Bob. "Plans Must Be Big and Broad: The Beginning of Recreation Planning on the National Forests." USDA Forest Service Pike and San Isabel National Forest Filed Manuscript.

Chronic, Halka. 1980. *Roadside Geology of Colorado*. (Missoula, MT: Mountain Press Publishing).

Colorado Mountain Club with Robert M. Ormes. 1992. *Guide to the Colorado Mountains.* Ninth Edition. (Denver, CO: Colorado Mountain Club).

"Colorado Trails Resource Guide: A Guide for All Trail Users." 1994. (Westminster, CO: Trail Mates of Colorado Publishing).

"El Paso County Regional Parks and Trails." March, 1994. El Paso County Parks Brochure.

Fry, Eleanor. *Pueblo County Historical Society, Pueblo Lore,* January 1982, 6-7.

Green, Stewart M. 1994. *Colorado Scenic Drives*. (Helena, MT: Falcon Press).

Illg, Gordon and Cathy. "Colorado Springs State Wildlife Area." *Colorado Outdoors,* March-April 1992, 24-25.

Kindle, Henry F. "The Marion Mine." *Pueblo County Historical Society, Pueblo Lore,* 17:1 (January 1992).

LeMassena, R.A. 1965. *Colorado's Mountain Railroads, Volume II.* (Golden, CO: The Smoking Stack Press).

Lentz, Martha J., Ph.D., R.N., Steven C. Macdonald, M.P.H., E.M.T. and Jan D. Carline, Ph.D. 1985. *Mountaineering First Aid.* Third Edition. (Seattle, WA: The Mountaineers).

Little, W. T., Jack McFall, et al. "A Look Back Into History." *Cañon City Daily Record,* (1972).

"Living With Wildlife in Bear Country." Colorado Division of Wildlife Brochure.

"Living With Wildlife in Lion Country." Colorado Division of Wildlife Brochure.

Malocsay, Zoltan. 2001 Revised. *Trails Guide: Denver to Pikes Peak.* Sixth Edition. (Colorado Springs, CO: Squeezy Press).

McCauley, Ella. *San Isabel, Colorado: Remembrance of Early Pioneers and Events of the Area 1845-1986.*

Ormes, Robert M. 1963. *Railroads and the Rockies.* (Denver, CO: Sage Books).

Ormes, Robert M. 1975. *Tracking Ghost Railroads in Colorado.* (Colorado Springs, CO: Century One Press).

O'Shaughnessy, Lynn. "Taking a Tick Check." *Friendly Exchange,* Summer 1995, 46.

Pueblo County Historical Society. "Carhart File."

Riddle, Michael J. 1992. "A Cultural Resource Survey of the Newlin Creek Trail Project, Fremont and Custer Counties, Colorado." Pike and San Isabel National Forests Files, Allen E. Kane, Principal Investigator: 10-11, 13-15.

Sease, John Joseph. Recorded by Ola Bigelow Plymell. "Stories of Pioneer Days in the Beulah and Pueblo Vicinity."

Smith, Kathy. "My Community, Early Days at Wetmore." (1982).

Taylor, Ralph C. 1963. *Colorado South of the Border.* (Denver, CO: Sage Books).

Thessen, Michael. 1993. *Trail Guide Wet Mountains.* (Pueblo, CO: Michael Thessen).

Williams, George. 1994. "Pueblo Mountain Park." Department of Planning and Development and San Isabel National Forest Files, Pueblo, CO.

NOTES

NOTES